747.092

THE
IMPATIENT
PEN

NICKY HASLAM

THE IMPATIENT PEN

Printed Matter

Observations,
Critiques & Tributes

by Zuleika Books & Publishing

Thomas House, 84 Eccleston Square, London, SW1V 1PX

British Library Cataloguing in Publication Data

A catalogue record for this book is
available from the British Library

ISBN: 978-1999623241

Typeset by Euan Monaghan

Printed in Great Britain by Clays Ltd.

Dedicated to the memory of Sybille Bedford

CONTENTS

A FOREWORD

A.N. Wilson

This collection of Nicky Haslam's occasional writings – sprightly, witty, utterly without self-regard – takes us from Eton in the 1950s, to the USA in the 1960s up to the present day. Nicky loves puns, jokes, gossip, but he is not malicious. He reflects on grand and famous people but he is not a snob. He finds class much too funny to take it with the seriousness that snobbery demands. He moves in the world, and loves the people he meets there, seeing the good in Princess Margaret, Norman Hartnell, Charlie Maclean, and bringing them to life for us. There's nothing judgemental in the following pages. That is such a very rare quality. Nicky Haslam is out of step with our fiercely puritanical, peevish times. It is the niceness of Noel Coward that he remembers. The Duchess of Windsor is praised for the dignified way she conducted her third marriage. Nicky knew them both well. He sees the point of Nigel Dempster , who was a very remarkable man, elevating gossip to something like art. Dempster was a divided self, a ruined angel, who half hated the fashionable world he loved to describe. Nicky is much gentler, much more self-confident and much, much cleverer. Both Nicky and Dempster however, saw that gossip was simply another word for finding other people, and the extraordinary world in which we find ourselves, interesting.

In a review of the truly gut-wrenching memoirs of Robert Montagu, – a book about being abused by his own father, the 10th Earl of Sandwich – Nicky notes with approval that Montagu blames no one, least of all himself. The quality Haslam most esteems in a brave, honest book, is its refusal to condemn those involved. The interview with Lee Radziwill makes me wish I were the editor of a newspaper. I would sign up Nicky immediately as a star interviewer – he brings her so vividly to life, her looks, her voice, her magic.

You could apply to this book the words he himself uses of Noel Coward : "Throughout this clever creation, paramount is its subject's sheer pleasure in living life". One would add that this author, like Noel Coward, is extremely funny. How lucky we all are that he exists.

In order to maintain the integrity of the author's writing, these works interchange between British and American English, as determined by their original publications.

VERBATIM *OR* HOW I JOINED UP NUMBER TWO AND NUMBER FOUR, HANS PLACE

A Monologue

Maureen, Marchioness of Dufferin and Ava

'Well, you see, I thought I ought to give a party for Princess Margaret – in the days when she was sweet – as I felt so upset about the bust-up with Peter Townsend. So I had arranged that she would greet the guests, a few of them my slightly older friends, but most of them hers, at the door with champagne to get her over her anxiousness and then the party would be in the ball-room, at little tables, so as to be completely informal.

But a few days before, Peter Coates rang up and said, 'Maureen, I know you'll be so pleased with me – last night I sat next to Princess Marina and I asked her to your party and she said she'd love to come. 'You can imagine my horror, after all it was arranged for Princess Margaret, and they all want to be the queen bee in the room, but Peter had done it, so of course then I had to invite Noel Coward and all Princess Marina's friends and it became two groups, with the absolute agony of not knowing how to divide them.

Clever Felix Harbord, who was then in my life, said, staring down at his thumb-twiddling hands, "there's a

1

flat roof outside your house, Number Four, and I think it belongs to the Chelsea Telephone Company so if I go nicely and ask them, maybe they might let you put a dance floor on it for the evening, for Princess Margaret's group."

Well of course the telephone people said yes, but then there was the problem of the windows of Number Two looking onto the party roof. But Felix said, 'oh it's very easy, we can just block out their windows for the night.' It may have been easy for Felix, but it was also easy for the dreary owners of Number Two to look through Felix's blocking out and they wrote a letter saying, "Lady Dufferin, we saw what was happening on that roof last night and wish to complain"....remember this was in 1952!

Well, the Number Twos went on being perfectly maddening about the whole thing, so the next time I had Princess Margaret to dinner I asked them to come and be photographed with her as she arrived. That did it. And when they wanted to sell Number Two, they offered it to me. I had an endless fight with Harrods but I won, and joined the two houses up. Lucky, as when I wanted to marry the Judge, I couldn't really put him in a slip, he had his own furniture and things, so he moved into this room, which, as you realise, having mountaineered up and down to it, is half-a-floor below my bedroom.

As I couldn't always be rushing along a corridor and downstairs to ask the Judge if I had time for a bath, or telephoning him, I asked Felix to make this speaking-tunnel between the two floors. "Do you really want to poke a hole between your two bedrooms?" Felix said. So of course it became known as the Poke-Hole.

Too funny, as if you look down it from Number Four, all you can see is somebody's horrid feet in Number Two, and if you look up it from there, you can only see the ceiling of my bedroom, but it did make communication with the Judge rather heavenly. And it's all due to Peter Coates's typically maddening interfering.'

This, and the following interviews in this book were conducted without recording.

NO LONGER WITH US

The Oldie

A review of *Encounters with Naim Attallah* by Naim Attallah

We all know about Daunt Books, but this one is truly daunting. Not due to its content, but oh dear, the weight. Ask Santa for a lectern. It's hardly the thing for the beach in Barbados, but its 850-odd pages will surely keep you head-down till winter's tail-end.

No-one who has ever come into contact with Naim Attallah could refuse his requests. There is something about the stoop, the darting eyes, the ears like smashed teapots, the glistening cranium that defies the answer no. And there's that faintly daffy expression and always the wildly colourful ties to put one at ease.

While all his publishing life he's commissioned books ranging from the frivolous to the instructive, his own have been manifestly intellectual. And Naim is not out to entrap; amused as he is by gossip, here it's far from his aim, though sometimes, happily, a bit creeps in. Meticulously researched, and elegantly put, his questions don't take his subjects aback, but lead to seamlessly flowing replies.

Horace Walpole believed there was 'no wisdom comparable...the babble of old people make one live back into the centuries'. Babble is hardly the mot juste for the answers Naim extracts from the dear departed in these lengthy interviews; perhaps Babel would be more appropriate, as many were clearly multilingual as well as older and wiser; none are evasive, many surprisingly frank, others throw new light on the people or circumstances of their lifetime. Some really read as potted autobiographies. And if a few get shirty at very penetrating questions they are asked, they are all patently honest, and there's hardly a bore among them.

These are in essence the last voices of the twentieth century (indeed some were born in the nineteenth), of individually thinking people, educated or not (some actually didn't go to school), before the mass mad rush to universities, and received opinions became the norm.

Attallah raises many issues – anti-Semitism, homosexuality in the Church, fascism, racial abuse, looming lesbianism and fading class, the flagrantly gay, the resolutely closeted – decades before they were thrust in their faces, and all the more interesting as the replies have not been already expressed anywhere else, and for not being trotted out by some glib, self-satisfied know-it-all.

The balance is roughly half writers, half the more stolid of professions, and shamelessly I turned first to the pages on people I had known, some whom I'd interviewed myself in the 1970s for the then fearfully trendy Ritz magazine and, of course, friends. We tend to think we have a better knowledge of our friends than anything an interviewer could prize out of them, but here are opinions, stances, analysis, historical details, humour and irreverence that greatly add to our perceptions, and bring back their physical presence, their voices, their foibles, their strengths. When reading the Sybil Bedford interview I was back in corner tables at proper restaurants, and her knowledge of everything from the temperature of the wine and the correct thickness of the soup to vivid experiences of almost every European country. Lord Lambton's showed the depth behind his darting conversation, and Arthur Schlesinger enlightened me on the decade I lived in the United States.

And while everyone given their voice in No Longer With Us is certainly very distinguished, they are not the usual gamut of the ultra-prominent who were so routinely puffed and profiled during those years. Thus, each is eminently worthy of being included in this record of 'living back' into former times of thought and wisdom, long pre-Internet, long before PC, trolling, mindfulness and self-pity. By so doing, Naim has, in this towering Babel, given those he encountered an enduring and endearing memorial.

BRENDA VACCARO

Ritz Magazine

She's staying at John Schlesinger's, her great friend since he directed her in 'Midnight Cowboy'. On the way to see her I'm thinking, she's the new type of American film actress – that's very different from 'Film Star'. She'll be serious, talk about meaning, and content, and probably look a mess.

The room is big and beige and at the moment lifeless. Not for long. An almost classic 'Film Star' entrance happens, blonde fur and Cal-tanned face, red-gold hair bouncing, a wide white smile and a ludicrously husky,

'Hullo, I'm Brenda. I'm sorry I'm late.'

She's not, as it happens, I'm early.

'Must just see if there are any messages.'

There are, of course.

Into telephone:

'Hi, it's Brenda. Okay, I'll hang on'.

To me:

'I don't usually talk in this dumb, come-on voice, you know. I got sick, like bad, two days after I got here. Hit me like a ton of bricks, and I'm still sick, and I gotta leave tomorrow whatever but John says I can't fly eleven hours non-stop without seeing a doctor first, so I'm going to see one this after — yeah?'

To telephone again:

'Yup, this is Brenda. Oh hi, Marleen, what's the play

we're seeing? Tonight. What? Fish? Dusa? Sounds weird.
What? About these women? I figured. Can't we go see
the Vienna Woods thing at the National? I hear the
production's great. You have? Oh great, fantastic. Come
right on over around 6.30 Marleen, you can see the
house, have a drink. Okay?'

Marleen and Brenda's evening is fixed.

'Like I was saying I got real sick and had to be in bed
forever, now I got so much to get done. I really only
came over here for two days to see about doing a film
with Davina Belling and Clive Parsons. They did 'Inserts',
great movie, see it? This one I'm doing for them is called
San Jose Mile, it's a wild comedy. Raquel Welsh plays
in it too. I love Raquel, she's a very funny, jokey lady,
great sense of humour. And I hope to do *The Muppets*.
I just loved it when I saw Lena Horne on it the other
day. It's fantastic, so well-constructed. But I was in bed
Tuesday, Wednesday, Thursday, Friday, Saturday, that's
five days, and now I just can't wait to get back, not that
I don't adore England, I was here in August and again in
November, but I miss my wonderful new house and my
animals and my birds and Tom Stroud, that's my feller…
look at that sunlight catching the rain, isn't that beautiful… because suddenly I feel my life changing. I mean
I was married some years ago for a minute and then I
was with Michael Douglas, Kirk Douglas' son, for five
years, but I never wanted children, and didn't think I
really wanted a marriage again. But then I met Tom one
and a half years ago… we were making *Death Weekend*
together up in Canada, and he saw me and I saw him
and he said simply, "I'm gonna' kidnap you", dead serious, and he did. Do you want a soda?'

She bounces out and into the kitchen.

'Fresca okay? Want ice?'

I look at my watch. I've been there all of six minutes. She bounces back.

'Tom's very direct, the directest person since me. He wants us to marry. He wants me to have his child. He says "what have you got to lose?" He's just got the lead in *Choirboys*, for Robert Aldridge. Fantastic part. But this change in me is a surprise to myself. I'm suddenly a very happy silly lady, I feel eleven years old. What time should I order a cab to get to Dr Patrick Woodcock? Oh God I hope I can fly tomorrow, though flying's not one of my most favourite things, and making *Airport 77* with Jimmy Stewart didn't help as I practically got pneumonia in the plane crashing into the sea scene. I could hardly believe working with Jimmy. Sometimes after a scene he'd give me a wink and a nod. That's worth a million bucks. Those pros, those survivors, wow. People like Katherine Hepburn, did you see her in Albee's *A Delicate Balance* last year? And Bette Davis! Now *Voyager* is my favourite film, that dialogue, that line: "Why ask for the moon when we have the stars?" And Kim Stanley. She's now teaching children English in New Mexico. Can you imagine being taught English by Kim Stanley?'

She lights a Marlboro and immediately stubs it out.

'I've been very lucky to work with such great people. And with Jack Lemmon, who's *Airport 77*. Jack's the sweetest man and so brilliant. All the people of his time are pretty wonderful. The new lot, well, they're kinda' mean and haven't got it right yet. Hollywood's got diversified. But we are lucky to have great young directors. John's my favourite, and Lindsay Anderson and Alan Pakula. I'd have loved to have worked for De Sica. I'd love to work for the National Theatre here, it's so civilised, there's a bar for the actors backstage. I was there the other day and had lunch with Gielgud. Sir John Gielgud, I couldn't believe it was me there. And then Paul Scofield came in. I mean... I guess I'm just a starfucker. Who isn't?'

Another Marlboro, another stub.

'I hope that cab's not gonna be late. I'm so sick of being sick. I have two weeks back home to really relax before I start work, and I'm working with people I don't really know too well, and I'm used to working with friends. Friends are like a family, especially in L.A. The great thing is the family seems to grow all the time. Television's rough and difficult, but it can be useful. My series *Sarah* was a disaster, the studio's still having arrested coronaries over the amount the costumes alone cost, but it had a guaranteed run and made me enough money to buy my beautiful house in Benedict Canyon. I can't believe that I've got a house on Benedict Canyon. I can see deer at the far end of the garden. Like the character I played in *Sarah*, I've gone West gradually. Only unlike her, I've found the beautiful perfect limit. I said to Olivia de Havilland, "Olivia I've done this dumb thing, I've bought this house" and she said, "My dear girl, every woman should have property, it's her only security. Buy property whenever you can in someplace you're happy." So, maybe, who knows, I may wind up buying a little place here, there are a lot of interesting things being done here.'

Telephone rings:

'Excuse me. Oh thanks Doreen. The cab's here, do you think I should keep him waiting while I'm at the doctor's? I mean it might be hard to pick one up at that time, you think?'

Not with your wide, white-smiling California tan, the bouncing red-gold hair, the blond furs, it won't. Not with your enthusiasm, infectious happiness, optimism. Brenda Vaccaro may be a film actress, but she's also not very far away from Bette and Olivia and Jack and Jim and Jimmy, the other thing.

CHARLIE MACLEAN

Ritz Magazine

He's having his photograph taken as he talks about his new book, *The Pathetic Phallus*, talking above the background noise of parrots screaming, Fred Astaire, dogs being let in or out (always too late). He says he's nervous, he often does but you wouldn't think it, this cat who's got three new books coming out this year, who looks cool as a Dayville's Frozen Yoghurt. One of the most beautiful girls in the world slides into the studio, strong men quake-material. Charlie's shaded eyes flicker over her, the jawline slightly constricts, as if, like some python, to swallow her whole. But he goes on talking, quietly, hesitating slightly.

'Oh God, I wish there were another word for porn... I mean if one talks about sex and sexual acts it's just talk. But the minute one either writes them down, or films them or whatever, it becomes this dreadful kind of crime. I love pornography, I love to read it, but it has to also make me laugh, not shudder. Any wanker who buys my book to get off on it, is out to lunch. I mean it's not in cellophane wrappers, though it probably will be in Soho bookshops.

The porn in my book is not there just to be that. Any porn that's there is to illustrate character more than action, and also to make a laugh. Laughter is a serious business... people talk about sex but don't yet laugh about it. Talk alone produces too much sexual content in daily life, which leads to sexual violence, which in turn leads to stuff like women's lib, which should be unnecessary. My book is maybe designed to worry men, which is why it's popular with women, but it also makes them worry, that they use men, and in the end they are guilty because they've got men worried. And the central figure, the attacker-attacked, is a Narcissus symbol, sympathetic and tragic... fundamentally it's a very classical format, out of the Greek legends, via Faust, Tennyson, Diderot; a kind of epic poem and comic strip. With porn thrown in. What more could you want?'

But because of that pornographic overtone, Charlie sweated out three years of the book being turned down by every big publisher, some however doing so:

'...because it wasn't pornographic enough or I hadn't detailed lurid perversion or sado-masochism, which I hate. There's one cutting up bit at the beginning, but it's an intended reminder of what I hope we've left behind in the degenerate scenes of the last decade. I can't stress too hard the intent of fun in the book... most new novels are a big fucking bore, dreary people in dreary Hampstead maisonettes clawing their way about, no wonder people don't buy the fucking things. The public's and critics' idea of novels hasn't moved an inch since, well, the thirties. I've heard bad reactions to my book in the halls of the BBC, macho media men only into drink and screwing... no smiles cracked there. Anyone who laughs reading my book becomes an automatic friend, or rather comrade.'

In spite of those sullen, sodden faces, no less than

six film companies, Hollywood among them, are after the rights.

'...which is odd, partly because as yet I haven't got an American publisher, and partly because most Americans are prudes, they really get sweated up if they are meant to laugh at sex. They like everything to be either cruel or cute. Which may be why I got a letter from an American film company about my next book, a clinical, factual study of children brought up by wolves in India, saying, "we don't feel the wolf children are sufficiently warm and loveable enough to traduce readily into commerce". I suppose they see some kind of Shirley Temple wolf-drag bullshit. I think *The Pathetic Phallus* might make a good film, with the right director. Roman Polanski maybe, or I'd be quite happy just to sell it and wash my hands of it. Whatever happens, I hope they get the point of it, that it's not designed to shock purely because it's pornographic.'

SIR NORMAN HARTNELL

Ritz Magazine

'Light is life' he said, throwing switches that illuminated the huge, crystal-hung, mirrored salon with an almost blinding brilliance. 'There are an awful lot of mirrors here I'm afraid. Do they bother you? – I must have light.' And so he must, this man who has put more lights onto fabric than any other couturier, and who brought light-heartedness into the art of dressmaking.

'When I started, all women except actresses were dressed in that severe so-called boyish way, you know, tubes to the knee and Eton crops. All dressmakers then wanted to make their clients, whatever class, look like society ladies. I wanted to make society ladies look like cocottes. To begin with, I've always thought that all frocks are prettier long, and I made a collection – all long – and took them to Paris. Baron de Meyer photographed them and the pictures came out in 'American Harpers' with the headline 'The most beautiful dresses in the world come from London, and are made by Hartnell'. That was nice, wasn't it? Then I started doing rather outrageous things like black velvet and monkey fur and enormous cartwheel hats... this was long before Dietrich had them, mind you. I've always loved black... I remember being in Buenos Aires staying at the Copacabana Hotel doing some black frocks for Eva

Peron, about six I think, and King Carol of Romania
had taken a whole floor of the hotel because his mistress Magda Lupescu was feeling a bit poorly. But she
knew I had a silver tissue wedding dress in my collection and sent down for it. She put it on, got a whole lot
of candles and lilies, lay down on the bed, then sent for
King Carol and told him she was dying. He said, "Oh,
please don't die, just as I was about to ask you to marry
me", and she sat bolt upright and said she felt much
better and wanted a cup of tea. I had to take the dress
downstairs and they never married. But it shows the
power of silver tissue.'

The lights were being adjusted now, the silver reflecting umbrellas fixed above the camera. 'Aren't those
pretty. Now look at that mirror vase, it's the same one
as in that photograph of Merle, filled with lilies… lilies and orchids, they were the flowers, until Constance
Spry thought up twigs. Everything was white then, or
beige, you know the Syrie Maugham and Elsie Mendl
thing, and I got rather tired of it and began to dye furs
pastel colours, lilac and pale green and things and it
caused a furore, people carried on as if it was sacri-
legious. But they caught on; Gertrude Lawrence, who
was certainly my favourite person to dress wore them
immediately, so did Leonora Corbett… she had such
style when she had very little money, but I last saw her
in Paris when she was being kept by one of the world's
richest men and the poor thing was dressed by… long
pause and eyes on the ceiling… GIVENCHY.

I go to Paris now on a busman's holiday, late on in
collection time and sit at the back. I love seeing other
peoples' work. But mostly I like places like Clacton,

you know, aspidistras and kedgeree... as you see really Paris comes to me, but I only mean that in the sense that endless French people bring sample cloth to me in London and all my fabrics are French except the wools which I always say are English. But I had some French customers... once the receptionist rang upstairs to say there was a Miss Tangay to see me... well of course it was Mistinguette, I made her a few frocks. Another was Alice Delysia, a real Parisienne, so beautiful, born Mlle Pizzy. Heavens she was a star... only Garbo and Alice Delysia are really worthy of that word... we were even engaged once for about ten days and the rumour got into the papers. I was going to see the Queen Mother, the then Queen Mother, Queen Mary, and one of her ladies telephoned me to know if the Queen would have to congratulate me on my engagement. I said I didn't really expect it to come off, and Queen Mary's lady said that's good because the Queen doesn't want to have to say she hopes it isn't true.

Queen Mary was a marvellous, forthright person, she used to go wandering about in the stockroom and workrooms with that funny cane with the duck's face on the handle, and talk to the girls... and there were a lot in those days, I used to have eighty-four embroiderers alone... and I think she was always a teeny bit jealous of all the lovely colours I was doing for the Queen – the Queen Mother – as she always stuck to greys and mauves because she was brought up in a world and time when courts dictated clothes and their colours. But when I did the Queen's trousseau for her state visit to Paris in 1938, she was in mourning for her father and felt it should all be black. Much as I love black I thought it would be *too* dull really so I said isn't white mourning a Royal prerogative, and it was so we did the whole thing again in sparkling white, every stitch. A month later I received a medal from the French Government, a kind of version of the 'immortelles' but for artists. It's their equivalent of a knighthood. That was rather nice, wasn't it? The King used to take me round picture galleries with a cigarette in his mouth and we would look at the Winterhalters and Hayters and he would say "I think these fashions would suit my wife the Queen", so you see the Royal Look that I am most identified with was really invented by them themselves.'

Now the mirrors are sparkling with the added lights of the flash. 'This is when I'm meant to say, have you taken it? Isn't it? Oh that polaroid is good, aren't they fast; you are a clever boy, you'll do quite well one day. Well, come and see the show tomorrow, most of it's dull selling stuff but I've done a few funny things as it's Jubilee year. Bring some interested friends, men or women, but *don't* bring a prospective client, I just can't handle any more work; I'm up to my eyes.'

He turns the lights off, gradually. The mirrors and chandeliers become dark, lustrous pools, dimly reflecting the man who for twenty-five years has dressed the most famous women in the world. It's not just *her* jubilee year. That's nice, isn't it?

PETER EYRE

Ritz Magazine

'Hi, Peter, oh God, Peter, how great to see you!' It was, in fact, Candy Bergen speaking, and it was lunchtime, and in San Lorenzo. People at lunch in San Lorenzo say lots of silly things, but I have been in many rooms and in many places when people have said to Peter Eyre 'Oh God, Peter, how great to see you', and the people who said it have not necessarily been anything more than just his friends, for he has a unique attitude to his friendships: sometimes tough, critical, always considerate. He says of his acting, 'one must try to be surprising without being frightening', and this could be the keynote to his substance.

Thing is, he has all the qualities many actors don't usually have, or don't need to have. He is tender, candid, and profoundly sympathetic to the problems of others. You will notice, says John Heilpern, that when magazines mention him they don't say *actor Peter Eyre,* but simply *Peter Eyre.* Perhaps that's because his form of acting is so underplayed. When you see him on stage, one is immediately aware that he is not Peter Eyre desperately trying to be someone else, but rather someone successfully being as every day and life-like as Peter Eyre… he himself says of his work, 'we are dealing with art, not fashion', and *Vogue* has quoted him as saying that he'd be flattered if 'someone mistook me for a Scandinavian student', both of which are apt, for, to mistake him for a student would be understandable, and he is, though fashionable and fashion-aware, completely unconscious of fashion in terms of the theatre.

On the face of it, that he should be an actor at all seems peculiar. If not actually rich, at least pretty few worries in that area: his main interests are music and opera, about both of which he knows more than most people in those fields today. Physically, too, his long, slightly ungainly frame and almost frivolous, un-intense demeanour don't exactly scream Hamlet or Constantin in one's ear. He seems almost blatantly English; Public School, University, aesthetic...

'Come on, I'm only quarter English, the rest some unbelievable mixture of German and Peruvian, and I was brought up mainly in America. I did go to an English Public School, a Roman Catholic one, though. That was a fate worse than life. It prepared one for nothing but being a cross between some kind of Malaysian tea planter and a Saint, two forms of morality that are in conflict with each other. Look at the schlepps that come out of most Public Schools.

... I would rather have chopped liver. I'll never understand quite why I went there, maybe my father felt that after a childhood of hotels and rented houses it would give me roots. Some roots! I loved living in hotels, still do, in fact I was born in one in New York, the Pierre, Room 1457. It's a broom closet now, I looked the other day. The only thing I remember about the Pierre was seeing Joan Bennett in the elevator. How did I know it was Joan Bennett, I was only about five. She'd just shot at somebody, or been shot at, was it Walter Wanger?

Later on I remember Central Park. The Park and
The Zoo. East-side exercise meant going to The Park,
and fun meant going to The Zoo. Amazing, that city
so vicious and so dirty had that zoo right there with
so many tame animals, and so many rich men's children gawping at them and eating crackerjacks and
watching actresses bicycling. I don't know who they
were but I remember then being told there's an actress
bicycling. And then once we rented a house in Aiken
South Carolina and I'd go for walks and see posters of
wanted outlaws. We were surrounded by forests lived
in by hunted animals and bandits. "Deliverance" is like
the South as I remember it then. I was sent to a school
called Portsmouth Priory. I loved it, it was in a wonderful position over the river, by the bridge that separates
Providence from Rhode Island. Run by a lot of monks,
one – the Latin teacher – had been a dancer in Pavlova's
touring company! That was where I first acted, I fell off
the stage at the first performance. After that, England
and Public School. I hated that, hated boarding. Boys
in America screwed the teachers and got drunk. But
English boys of the same age were suffering themselves
with Bath Buns. My twin brother and I felt our adulthood, so severely acquired, was being insulted.

By this time I was the biggest opera bore in history. I can still recall the first time I felt glamorised... it
was listening to Helen Traubel on the radio. But I kind
of forgot that in England, and didn't train or anything
so after leaving school I did the next best thing and
went to an audition at the Old Vic where I lied to the
director, said I'd studied in Paris. He made me do three
speeches in English and I was just *so* bad, then he said,

trying to catch me out, do something in French, and I
happened to have learned a piece of Racine, so I did a
speech from Andromache, waving my arms about like
mad and it was OK.'

It certainly was OK. From then on Nottingham Rep,
The Royal Court, *Ghosts*, *Three Sisters*, *Seagull*, *Hamlet*,
films... currently running is the best screen version of
Hedda Gabler, which he played world-wide with the
present co-star in *Stevie*, Glenda Jackson. When that
run finishes he's off to some nice hotels in America,
and 'God, Peter, how great to see you'.

OLD KING NOËL

The Spectator

A review of *The Treasures of Noel Coward: Star Quality* by Barry Day

W hat is this I hold in my hands? Is it just a book? It's quite heavy, but somehow, instinctively, one feels its light heart. When I eventually prize its even glossier inner core from its glossy padded outer shell, I still ask: what is this? It looks like a book, but its pages don't shut flat or lie open; they spring apart, gaping enticingly, as if someone had inserted bulky, once-essential memos or long-forgotten mementos between the pages. But shake it, and nothing falls out. No shopping list, no ribbon-tied bundles of unrequited love, no scrunched up scraps of half-remembered receipts. Open it at one of these many inviting gaps. What's this? A manila envelope, seemingly casually inserted, but integrally attached to the right-hand page. Lift the flap, draw out the contents. What can they be?

There can't be much left to say about the subject of this elaborate compendium; but by creating so novel a volume on Noël Coward's trawled-over life and talent, Barry Day has come up with the goods. The manila envelopes contain facsimile documents of the rise of Destiny's 'Tot to Total Adoration to Nation Indebted'.

They show that from his nativity (copy of the certificate recording that blessed event included) in Teddington, then a leafy suburb a mere crow's-flight from the tinkly West End waltzes of *The Dollar Princess* or *Maid of the Mountains,* Noël Coward was a living cert to take 'thear-tah' by the throat and stuff his perception of modern life down it.

His progress, from playing fairy sunbeams via writing sentimental semi-operas, or drug-fuelled youthful declines, the gayest of comedies, the brittlest of revues — often starring himself – to more maudlin late flops about fearful senility, has been thoroughly documented; but the ephemera included in this book – letters from Mountbatten, lyrics for Marlene, far-flung journeys and star-crossed casts – give the Master's life a lasting, tactile dimension.

He always knew – 'I have star quality' boasted this oddly least boastful of luvvies. He could hold an audience, on stage or off, by sharp one-liners only matched by Groucho Marx or on one occasion, Edna Ferber. Seeing the pinstripe-suited authoress, Noël said: 'Goodness, Edna, you look almost like a man!' Miss Ferber replied: 'So do you, Noël.'

His plays, his tunes and lyrics are now folkloric, and if the former are unavoidably dated these days, the latter have an everlasting, utterly English poignancy (*'Somewhere I'll Find You'*) or a kind of Wodehousian, deprecating humour ('The Stately Homes of England'). In his outlook, he seems somewhat parochial compared to the worldly sophistication of his nearest rival, Cole Porter. Though Porter was richer, better dressed, had better taste and wrote bigger hits, Noël showed no envy towards him, but acknowledged such talent by writing that Nina from Argentina, a grumpy Latino lass who refused to dance the beguine, 'cursed the man who taught her to. She cursed Cole Porter too.'

If he had no taste in decoration — his houses were for the most part banal — Coward certainly knew how to choose friends. He was a sucker for royalty, Prince George, Duke of Kent specifically, and the Duke's sister-in-law Queen Elizabeth before and after she became Queen Mother. And he always had a close coterie of other intimates whom he cherished. An illuminating side of the text shows that while fawned on by major stars, and later, even, when fading himself, he never deserted the friends of his youth. The letter from Daphne du Maurier describing her last days with their mutually beloved, dying Gertrude Lawrence – Coward's co-star in his earliest successes – is particularly touching. His loyalty was unbounded, sometimes even detrimental, such as the fruitless determination to make Graham Payne, the boy he was mad about, into a major star.

But throughout this clever creation, paramount is its subject's sheer pleasure in living life; from the smiling ingénue's eyes under a silk hat to the last photograph, a quizzical wrinkled moon face at his easel in Jamaica, his essential 'niceness' is evident.

SIR HAROLD ACTON

Ritz Magazine

Perhaps, because one knows Sir Harold Acton lived the 1930s in China, that he reads, writes and speaks Chinese, that he has written about Pekin so perfectly, one tends to detect a touch of the Buddha in those eyes, the head set so precariously on a forward-tilting body, an oriental finesse in the elegantly chosen words, in the voice with its rising cadence to end every sentence. There is for sure a mandarin quality about him, but in reality, it is not Eastern. Noble English blood, equally mixed with equally noble Italian, and straight-forward Chicago stock in his composition. Most famous now for his aesthetic Memoirs, his major work has been Western history, the documentation of Renaissance and Baroque Italian princes and statesmen...

'I'm currently working on a book about the Pazzi plot, a plot to murder Giuliano Di Medici and Lorenzo The Magnificent in Florence Cathedral. Pazzi only achieved the killing of Giuliano and got away with a wound in his neck, here, his neck. One of his friends sucked the blood from the wound in case the sword had been poisoned, which was perfectly likely. It sounds melodramatic, but it's all there, documented. Originally I had thought of it as a novel, but no, history is too eloquent, too strong...'

For half a century, like his father before him, the deity has been enthroned in La Pietra, his Florentine villa, a vast house surrounded by clipped allées, statues, pleasure grounds erected by mortal toil against olive and cedar, the blue and gold Tuscan sky above, the gold and blue Medici domes below. Inside the house is dark, cool, with damasks glowing onto the varnish of invaluable paintings.

'The best were stolen recently. The police found some of them. In a wood. What a place to leave a work of art... in a wood! Now I've had an alarm installed. It goes off if a dragonfly passes'.

... and the volumes of his invaluable library cascade from shelves onto tables that are loaded with signed photographs of Royalty...

'...they are the most persistent. They seem to expect one to be always around to entertain them' – and the objects of an intellectual lifetime, from D'Annunzio, from Evelyn Waugh, Graham Greene, Eleonora Duse... 'Duse! She wanted to move into my house. She had one of her own, but she said it was 'una casa di dolore, casa di pianto', so she wanted to live in mine. I couldn't have that. Florence used to attract the most extraordinary women... Mabel Dodge, Gertrude Stein. It still does, I fear. I live in dread of those literary ladies. They pursue one relentlessly'.

Yet, surprisingly, at the point when the period of his youth is coming into sharp scrutiny, when all his literary friends are being re-assessed...

'Over accessed. I have no nostalgia for my early youth in London. It was a very bleak period. What was there? Bloomsbury I suppose, but luckily I was on its very fringe. Virginia was so hideous! And all their voices, Virginia's in particular. Their enthusiasm was so overdone. They would enthuse over the slightest thing. If a cat, a little cat came into the room, it would be 'Look at that wondrous cat!' I can't think why the young are so interested by them. Every page of every English paper carries reams about the Woolfs! It will be the Sitwells' turn next. That new book on them is very good in a chatty way, and quite enough, but I suspect we are in for a deluge of the minutest works. Osbert wrote beautifully, and he had many odd characters to draw on. Sashie writes brilliantly, as he talks, and sees... to be somewhere with Sashie is an extraordinary experience, the mind is never dulled, he notices everything he is passing, even at a run, and remembers. But don't forget, Geoffrey Scott's *Architecture of Humanism*, one of the most perfect books of this century, came out long before Sashie's.

...but are not the diaries of that generation interesting?

'You must listen. I've told you that I am not interested by recent events. If I were, I would be full of the diaries of Mary Berenson, Mrs Bernard Berenson, which I have read, and which are very scandalous. She describes seeing Winnaretta De Polignac saddling up Violet Trefusis and riding her round a salon in Paris. In Paris! With a whip! That would interest the wife of a lugubrious writer on the restoration of English houses! I expect Mary Berenson's diaries will be published quite soon...'

Far away the bells of innumerable churches ring out their massive tones. Sir Harold inclines his head... 'two more of these excellent whiskies, please. Thank you so much... just a soda. Thank you. You see, if people don't follow the established religions, there's going to be a great deal more of such indecencies as the Guyana horror. Even in this country. Don't make the mistake of imagining it's a Californian phenomenon. I read that the Maharishi has bought Mentor Towers. The people he so called 'instructs' will need something more, a little more, a little jab, to listen to his ramblings. The great religions are so superbly simple. So simple... And now I must leave for dinner'.

And I should explain that we are not in Florence, not at La Pietra, but in the piano-bar of a small Mayfair hotel. As he puts on his hat and coat, Sir Harold sings part of 'The song is you'. He goes out into the London night, and stepping into the taxi, turns back: 'We were speaking earlier of Gertrude Stein, She was a monumental massive creature... dressed by Balmain. It was no credit to Balmain'.

The God is human.

MICHAEL WISHART

Ritz Magazine

Michael Wishart: Romantic recluse, spellbinding raconteur, tender friend, lyric painter, whose brush has consumed many dreams.

Michael Wishart: Snob, cynic, overindulgent hedonist, outrageous gossip, whom Kenneth Anger has called 'a goblin who lives under a bridge'.

If there are two sides to every answer, what, as Gertrude Stein said, is the question? Wishart's was how to enmesh his two vastly different sides into a book, *High* Diver, the autobiography of his youth and early manhood. It ends aet thirty-three. Why? 'It might have got boring.' That, almost certainly not. Nevertheless, to write an autobiography if one is not exactly a world-famous figure, is, these days, a challenge only a brave few would have the courage to meet. Was he nervous about writing such a self-revealing book?

'Not a bit, no. I was much more frightened with my first painting exhibitions. I was very young and very ambitious, but luckily I didn't get bad reviews, at least not for a bit, and when I did I thought they were amazing. I read them again and again.

But then I like seeing my name in print.

So with the book I wasn't worried; after all I am a painter first and an amateur writer second, and as such I was simply trying to chart a decade that hasn't yet been really touched on. Many people say the book is worth itself for pinpointing this particular period. Almost everyone has said the book is badly constructed. Well, all I can say is I wrote some chapters when I was twenty, others after thirty, and the rest in little scraps scrounged from diaries and letters written and unwritten.

You know, they are the ones one remembers most clearly, the unwritten, unsent letters.

Cyril Connolly, who was a very close friend and in love with my wife... when we were first married he resented me, that's in the book... but afterwards he often said "One day you must write a book. Your letters are among the few I save, they are as vivid as Byron's", so when we knew Cyril was dying I tried to put something together for him to read. Unfortunately, or perhaps fortunately, he was never able to.

Then later I lent the manuscript to Christopher Gibbs, who happened to have a publisher staying one weekend, and this publisher read them and rang me at four in the morning saying 'you're one of the few people who have what publishers look for like hounds look for truffles, the ability to put words and images together vividly.'

Robert Lowell told me he used a quotation for one of his poems from a letter of mine describing how sexual Sonia Henje's little white fur knickers and sharp bladed boots were to my childhood dreams.

So since I'd heard it from a professional publisher, I just tried to tidy up the manuscript. I wanted my prose to be like a shower of silver knives.

I know the shape has come out as I intend, but

certain reviewers don't see it in the same way. For instance, however hard one tries not to, one can't actually help noticing when, as an unknown writer, one gets three-quarters of a page review in the most prestigious literary magazine and even if it is written by someone whom I'm told detests me, it does seem rather strange that the reviewer accuses me of factual inaccuracy, particularly as he himself describes David Hockney and Patrick Proctor's line drawings of me as paintings.

I mean if you can't tell a line drawing from a painting I don't think you should waste a whole paragraph on art criticism.

Other critics, like George Melly, seem to have got the point – that I *was* trying to write a sad 'High Bohemian Jennifer's Diary'. I was lucky enough to know many extraordinary people, and I can't help it if my friends were the kind loathed by Puritans. Puritans loathed Denham, Denham Fouts.

He was everything you weren't meant to be, then, including beautiful and a man.

His circle of friends, Jean Cocteau, Bebe Berard, Jean Marais, was the most notorious of an already decadent group. I hear Truman Capote's new book is largely about Denham.

I remember Truman coming to the apartment in Paris, aged about nineteen, this American wonderboy. Denham was lying on the bed, plastered in makeup, filled with opium, surrounded by objects that his late majesty of Greece, or even Tredegar and Peter Watson had given him. Truman was very pretty, like a child, he had a fringe brushed forward – the hair went very early;

coming out of the bath you would think it was a tennis ball. Anyway, he was a very pretty and very talented tennis ball. He sat on the end of the bed, appalled by the decadence. "You mean to say you take drugs?" he mouthed. He didn't realise it was far too late to lecture Denham. Drugs were Denham's breath by then.

George Melly is right. I am elitist. I'd like the world to be peopled only with beautiful boys and intelligent friends, the ones I admire especially like Cyril, or Caroline Blackwood.

My cousin, Lady Caroline Blackwood. Her novels and short stories are so hauntingly brilliant.

Cecil Beaton is the most aesthetically sympathetic person I have ever known. It meant more to me than anything else when he began buying my work. He came round one day and looked at each of my paintings for about a minute and a half and then left. I was terrified that he hadn't liked any of them, but the next day he sent round perfect miniature diagrams of each painting, everything exactly placed – it was all embedded on his mind – with a note on one saying 'this is it, bring it soon', and a cheque. It was a portrait of an incredibly beautiful Arabic football player called Tij-Nani.

I first saw Tij-Nani sleeping in a park wearing only white satin football shorts, his head turned back into a clump of white hydrangeas. It was a donné. Later he came to stay with me. He used to come to bed with his football – a kind of talisman to him – and embrace it all night.

When I next saw that picture, hanging between the most wonderful Berard ever painted and my favourite Larry Rivers, and the best Tchelitchew on another wall,

I was astounded. It does give one a boost. But Cecil is an incredibly important influence as much in his writings as anything else. His prose may not be flawless but in a hundred years' time if anyone wants to know what went on between the upper classes and Bohemia they will turn to Cecil's diaries, not Cyril Connolly's opinion of whether Hemingway was worse than Scott Fitzgerald. His travel books, too, are fascinating reading even to anyone not interested in fashion or society. Cecil has been wonderfully helpful to me recently, researching material for the huge triptych I'm painting for Langan's Restaurant. At least I'm not actually painting it, as I particularly don't want it to be a big bad painting by Michael Wishart, so I looked for someone who I felt would be able to paint it through me, which might give it a slim chance of its being good. I couldn't find anyone for a long time, then suddenly I saw this boy.

I think one can be re-acclimatised to falling in love. It happens before you see the person. It's happened to me once before. This new one is vaguely touching that area where you're told not to by your conscience, which means I've got to, doesn't it? Why did Eve eat the apple? Not because there wasn't any other fruit in the garden – there may have been a hamper from Fortnum and Mason at her feet for all we know – but because she was told not to. I felt I was in love with this young man before he came into the room.

By some magic he can't paint, so he's doing the triptych on my instructions... I hate going up high ladders, anyway I love looking up at Johnny Mayberry on one. I found an extraordinary photograph of Toulouse Lautrec dressed as a Japanese emperor, this is the centre panel, and on the right is Barbette, who was a French transvestite tightrope-walker of immense beauty... not French actually, but a Texan boy.

From my favourite place, the wrong side of the tracks.

He is to be dressed in great glittering fake diamonds. My great admired friend Anton Dolin has Barbette's love letters, and I think he may do a book of them.

The third panel is to be – well I thought if I'm having one human midget dressed as a mikado, one hermaphrodite dressed in diamonds, I'd better have something really normal so I chose a negress.

Josephine Baker, whom I knew and loved. Maybe I will just have her wearing the little feathers she sometimes wore. You too know where I could get feathers? I went to buy Barbette's glitter in a shop off Oxford Street, and you know I bumped into at least seventeen Saint Nicholases on that one street.

I know that saints aren't too good at appearing when they are needed, but isn't it rather showing off to appear so often on one street? Isn't one getting slightly sick of... I mean, women who go to the races knowing not to wear what the one next to them is wearing... but those Saint Nicholases in their red dressing gowns trimmed with Tampax, haven't we seen it all too often? These sad figures plodding up and down and ringing their bells and robbing little children. I don't know where Saint Nicholas's reputation for being a benevolent chimney sweep comes from; he never seemed to come in my direction often. However, no matter what we forgive him because he is a stocking freak, and one can forgive them anything'.

STEPHEN TENNANT

Ritz Magazine

Half buried in one of those Wiltshire valleys that are like winding tunnels of dank, dark green stands an Elizabethan manor house, its overgrown gardens anchoring it inexorably to earlier foundations. Cut your way through the bolted, thorny roses, tear at tendrils of creeper that entwine an iron bell pull. It jangles surprisingly near, loudly. Then a long silence; are they still here, still asleep? Has the hundred years not yet passed? But wait, footsteps. Inside, you will find beauty, if not sleeping, certainly resting.

For this is the world of the Hon. Stephen Tennant, writer, poet, artist and last link with a gilded baroque generation of friends that included Osbert Sitwell, Siegfried Sassoon, Rex Whistler. When Stephen's famously beautiful mother, Lady Glenconner, married Lord Grey of Fallodon, Stephen came to live with her in this house, turning it into a focal point of aristocratic, artistic talent. Lady Grey decorated the house in the mode of the moment, sombre grand French, and after her death in the early thirties, Stephen made several startling rococo additions, masterminded by his great friend, Syrie Maugham. From that moment nothing, neither decorator nor duster, has touched it. David and Marie Bailey and I went to spend an afternoon there. I had prepared them for a surprise of bizarre originality. They were not even half prepared.

A nice old body with a good Wiltshire burr opened the door. 'Mr. Stephen's upstairs, resting.' (I told you so.) 'He says will you go up to his room?'

The hall always takes one's breath. Pink velvet swags cover what walls aren't painted with gold stars on powder blue, a gleaming silver ceiling, turquoise fur rugs over white fur rugs over fraying Aubusson. White and gilt carved rope furniture with white leather uphol-stery draped with vivid Chinese shawls and red Indian blankets. Light struggles out from crystal brackets or hollowed shells layered with cobwebs... 'you know his bedroom, don't you sir? On the left at the top of the stairs'... the stairs... On each long low tread are groups of objects, artlessly, carefully arranged. Broken lacquer fans, glass bowls of face powder, playbills of Sarah Bernhardt, topaz and ruby bracelets, lengths of ribbon and swan's-down, sheet music of Mistinguette, cheap coloured postcards of South Sea sunsets and black and white ones of the boxer Charpentier, matinee idols, actresses, ropes of pearls, empty boxes of Cadbury's Milk Assortment. One treads gingerly but the dust still swirls.

'Stephen?'

'I'm here dear, in my room, do, do come in. I'm resting, a touch of neuralgia, I think. I got it in Bournemouth. Do you ever go there? Such lovely shops. Yes, do come in and sit down. So sweet of you to come but I'm afraid I shall have to lie here and be quite quiet. I do think that after a certain age one should stay quite, quite

quiet. And who, dear, are these enchanting people you
have brought with you? How pretty they are.'

Stephen is lying fully dressed on what is not only an
unmade bed, but also his desk and his drawing board,
with his piles of many books that he constantly reads
and refers to. Some are by him, many by Willa Cather,
the great American novelist who was one of his dearest
friends, and to whose collected works Stephen wrote
the superb introduction. There are photographs and
postcards and prints, travel brochures and movie magazines, talismans that make this reclusive memory and
imagination soar to fantastic realms and places. He has
seen the world, seen through the world, from here. His
surprise at its beauty and fallacies are undimmed. He is
also an entrancing host.

'This is David and Marie Bailey, Stephen.'

'What pretty names. Welcome, welcome, and do sit
down. Are you brother and sister? No? Husband and
wife! How thrilling! You both look as if you had a touch
of the east about you, have you Mr Bailey? Oh, you were
born in India, so exciting, the mysterious Orient. And
you, dear Mrs Bailey?... Hawaiian and Japanese? Too
wonderful. I must show you my paintings of Hawaii.
No, I've never been there. But I can see it all, the sunsets, the coral reefs, the palm trees. I adore palm trees,
don't you? I've planted several in my garden, but I'm
afraid they go brown very quickly. Rather like me. I'm
very brown from this wonderful summer we've had. I
don't notice rain, do you, Mrs Bailey?'

He starts to stop resting, gathering up various bags
and shawls, books and photographs he always carries,
piling up his waist-length red-tinted hair, selecting rings

from the glittering recesses of several jewellery cases, neuralgia gone with the whirlwind of talk.

'What have you been doing, Stephen?'

'I've been looking after some lizards. Such sweet creatures. Do you like lizards, Mr Bailey? You look as if you did, we must see them after tea. Dear Nicky, do find Mrs Woodley and ask her to bring tea. Next door, I think, I'm feeling so much better I will lie on that sofa and afterwards you can show them the other rooms. Yes, they are pretty rooms, aren't they? Come along and sit here, Mrs Bailey, but, oh, Mr Bailey, don't take photographs of me! Has Mrs Bailey ever been photographed? What a lovely face you have. Do you have a career, or don't you want one? Mrs Bailey, I used to be beautiful like you, can you see that? I used to be *so* beautiful... it's a thing we can never stop being, can we? You must never stop, and I will never stop: we'll be beautiful always. But we won't enquire each other's ages.

Look at this photograph of me. It was a dress I had made all of gold ribbons, loose from the neck to the hem, so when I danced, the ribbons formed a gilded cage around me. We used to have ballets there on the lawn. And this photograph, me when a young man, a mere boy, really. How boyish young boys look, don't they? I had my mother's pretty chiselled nose... but I get so weary of my dreary face and we all look better with a little makeup, a little banana makeup. I saw a pantomime in Bournemouth not long ago and all the actors wore banana paste on their faces. I thought it too lovely. And we all need the dye-pot too, but of course it has to be beautifully done. My tea has gone ice cold as

usual. My friends tell me I do nothing but sit drinking
ice cold tea... so funny of them. Yes, do please look at
those paintings, they are quite recent ones, and they
are selling very well. Isn't it silly? I'm just going to fetch
something which may amuse you all.'

The paintings cover the floor, and every available
surface of the furniture. Totally original in style, in their
vibrant iridescent coloured inks, smouldering-eyed
Marseillaise sailors with mouths like crushed roses, or
flirtatious soubrettes in vast hats, glow among exotic
flowers and night-sky stars, the names of which...
Vega, Orion, Cassiopeia, Venus... Stephen delights in
(and uses often in his poems) and has written around,
with exquisite writings. Their theme has not changed
any more than the house, but has if anything, become
brighter, bolder, more fantastic and courageous. Like
the executor, who rejoins us, changed into an electric
blue shirt and some very short, and very baggy, shorts.
His legs, which are mahogany in front, are milk white
at the back.

'Aren't they a good colour? Just that cream, Ambre
Solaire. Nothing else. I've Mistinguette's legs. Second
to none! Now this, this is Mexico! A hammock made
in Mexico! Look at the colours... much better than my
legs! And this turquoise ring. That's Palm Beach. I can't
understand how I've never lost it. I lose everything. Or
they disappear in other ways. My dear old Nanny used
to say, '...if you have lovely things, you can't expect
people not to covet them'. Do you like this pink scarf,
Mrs Bailey? May I give it to you? It looks lovely with
your colouring. We must give and we must receive.
Sarah Bernhardt said that it's only by spending that

you gain anything. It's very profound – she was a mystic, there's no doubt. Look at this brooch! "Tendres pensées." Only the French could make that, couldn't they? They are comic, the French people, really. They shock and amuse one at the same time. Come along.'

The momentum is gathering. We follow Stephen, now burdened with the hammock, rings, ice-cold-tea cup into another room, of which the theme is black lace over white satin. He sits down and resumes as abruptly as he had left off.

'That rock crystal. It's the largest ever found in the Alps. And Syrie Maugham put this white rope round the cornice. Doesn't it go well with the Tudor ceiling? She used a lot of colour in this house, most unlike her. She said colour in the country made the silence sing, and I agree with her. I love the solitude and the silence. And now I must rest my throat. Silence. I want to be a mystery. All beauties should be mysterious'.

He means it. As we follow him from room to room, exclaiming at each new exotic vista, at the dining room ceiling covered in shells, we try to make him go with his unique flow of conversation, but Stephen keep his fingers pressed to his lips. Like all good givers, he knows when to stop. To him, after all, this unbelievable house is simply home, and his extraordinary lifestyle ordinary to him. He brushes off compliments and admiration with the good manners of an Edwardian hostess. Suddenly it's time for him to retire into his self-enchantment.

'I wish I could ask you all to stay the night, but I expect you are busy. I must rest... this horrible neuralgia, it makes me so dull, so dull to be with. I loved your bringing dear David and Marie, I'm sure they are difficult to pin down, always travelling. That's the trouble with the nicest people, they're always travelling. We won't say goodbye. Thank you for giving me so much pleasure. Thank you, thank you,' floats down from the darkness above the stairs, 'thank you...'

The front door shuts. Outside it's cold and wet. Of course Stephen never notices rain. It doesn't rain in dreamland.

SINGING COLE PORTER: 'I'VE GOT YOU UNDER MY SKIN'

The Oldie

Saint-Germain-des-Prés, summer 1958. The Chinese statues in Les Deux Magots nod sagely at the existential epigrams of Simone de Beauvoir; the jukeboxes blare Dalida's 'Garde-moi la Dernière Danse', les yé-yés writhe to Le Twist.

And, almost subliminally, everyone, young or old, in the streets, on the boulevards, in bistros and boudoirs, is singing 'I Love Paris', Cole Porter's newest and most haunting of tributes to the city he adored above all others. We heard it constantly, night and day.

I'd known it for a year or two already. Friends brought back from New York the new-fangled LPS – vinyl, not easily shattered shellac. Among them was the soundtrack to *Can-can*, Cole's latest Broadway triumph, and its subject was... well, Paris, in the 1880s. I'd even been taken to see the London production, hypnotised by its Lautrec-inspired sets, colours and *sans-culottes*. The leading lady sang 'I love Paris...' – against a scrim, 19th century map of the city, dark streets defined by pinpoints of lamplight that gently faded to a lilac, dawn sky, encircling Eiffel's newly-built tower – '...because my love is near'. Now I was in Paris, too.

Jaded youth that I was, I knew many of Cole's famous songs long before *Can-can*: 'Night and Day', 'Begin the

Beguine', 'I get a Kick out of You', 'I've Got You under my Skin'... The songs were grist to my mother's mill of rolling up the carpet – in the bedroom, where I lay immobile with polio – and, as Cole neatly put it, 'punishing the parquet' with a quick foxtrot.

Bedbound and able only to listen, I realised quite early on the immense subtlety of words and music this rich, spoiled, well-educated farmer's son from Peru, Indiana, could conjure. Later, I notice the in-jokes of 'Ridin' High' – 'What do I care if Countess Barbara Hutton has a Rolls Royce built for each gown?' – the historical references, and the shaded sexuality of, say, 'Love for Sale'.

I'd been told about Cole, and his famously beautiful wife Linda, their costume balls at the Ca' Rezzonico each Venetian season, their house in the Rue Monsieur, her clothes, his clothes, their style. I read Kenneth Tynan's essay in *Persona Grata*, beside Beaton's portrait of Cole, of how, at the Ritz bar, someone had given – to the man who has everything – a pair of gold sock suspenders. Thanking them effusively, Cole surreptitiously slipped off the gold sock suspenders he was already wearing and gave them to the barman. I knew of his band of friends – les Coleporteurs. And, of course, I read about his fall in 1937, riding at the Piping Rock Club, when the weight of his fallen horse crushed his legs to smithereens.

For many years to come, Cole Porter was the only person I really wanted to meet. So, it appears, did Khrushchev. When the old Soviet blocker paid his one and only visit to Hollywood, he insisted on being taken on the set of the filming of *Can-can*, where he was bussed on the mouth by its bright young star, Shirley

Maclaine. Cole was by now living largely in California, adapting his songs for the movies. But he often came to New York, to stay in his Billy Baldwin-decorated apartment on the 33rd floor of the Waldorf Towers. We had a mutual friend.

Jean Howard was a Texan beauty, born and bred with all the generosity of that state's natives. I'd met her in London, and now saw much of her in Manhattan. Her history is remarkable: ex-follies girl, occasional film star, Marlene's lover, obsession of Louis B. Mayer, wife of *the* leading agent Charles Feldman, and a brilliant photographer.

But this is Cole's story, not Jean's; though Cole was, I feel, always a little in love with her, as indeed was I. I badgered her endlessly about him. So, one day, she said, 'Well, you better meet him.' She arranged for me to be asked to dinner in the Waldorf Towers.

On the way, she prepped me. 'We will be shown into the library. Cole won't be in the room. He will be carried in...' – both legs useless now – 'So turn away, don't watch...'.

I sneaked the occasional peek, and saw this Mandarin-like figure, carried in burley arms, being arranged on a sofa, razor-sharp creases tugged perfectly, the tiny feet crossed, the carnation placed just-so. And then the voice, the signal to turn. 'My dears, would you like a Gibson?'

I was to hear that voice, and see the neat obsidian head, fairly often over the next year. His secretary Madeleine Smith would call me at *Vogue*.

'The Little Man [her code name for him] wants to know if you're free tomorrow evening?'

Was I ever? and always. Sometimes, there would be one or two old friends – more, too tiring – more often, we would be alone; the same ritual, the initial Gibson, before an elegant dinner on his Capodimonte porcelain. He'd want to hear about the Fonteyn/Nureyev season, about my friendship with Andy Warhol, about any of the friends he so rarely saw, that I'd run into. He'd encourage me to sing his – and other writers' – songs, now and then humming or, faintly, joining in.

There was a deep subtlety to his work that I'd imbued all those years ago, its grace and charm ever more compelling. Of all the great writers of the American songbook, only he – and his rival and friend Irving Berlin – needed no collaborator to create these masterpieces. There was no feeling about him of being world-weary or disillusioned by the passing of that world.

Though, one evening, we sang something, perhaps significant, from his final creation, a television musical of Aladdin starring Sal Mineo.

'Wouldn't it be fun not to be famous? Wouldn't it be fun not to be rich? Wouldn't it be pleasant to be a simple peasant and spend a happy day digging a ditch?'

Cole asked me for a weekend at his house in Williamsburg. I never saw him again. A few days later, he was taken to hospital, and then to California, where he died a year later, in 1964, aged seventy-three.

THE WALLIS SIMPSON I KNEW

The Spectator

A review of *Wallis in Love: The Untold True Passion of the Duchess of Windsor* by Andrew Morton.

One would have thought this particular can of worms might, after nearly eighty years, be well past its sell-by date. But books about Mrs Simpson and her infatuated king appear with thudding frequency, each with some ever more far-fetched theory about this curious union. Now comes the leaden hand and leaden prose of Andrew Morton, with yet another: that Wallis was, all her life, in love with another man long before, during and after her experience of vitriolic abuse, first as the besotted prince's obsession, then scapegoat for his abdication, and object of vilification during her years as his wife.

This love (to borrow words from her great-step-nephew, 'whatever love is') may well have been real. The man in question was Herman Rogers. The scion of an aristocratic family, he was educated at Yale where he was a 'Bones man' – the highest recognition of pure decency that institution can bestow – and handsome and rich to boot, and therefore certainly attractive. He was also artistic, gentle, kind and generous – and long married to a woman with whom he shared entire and mutual happiness. It's not, therefore, unlikely that Mrs Simpson, even when still the wife of the alcoholic, cruel Win Spencer, may have seen Rogers as an exemplar for a platonic liaison. One can be in love with people one esteems.

But in this meretricious book, Morton claims that all along it was Rogers she desired sexually. Attributed sources (a rarity for Morton) for this laughable premise are scant; Rogers's step-granddaughter, one Barbara Mason; and a Kitty Blair, his stepdaughter-in-law. Neither was close or old enough to be a witness and, fatally, they contradict each other on the very same page. Blair tells Morton that Wallis 'was never intimate with Herman', but two paragraphs earlier Mason claims that she 'wanted to try a different type gene-pool for the father of her child'. In the index, this is brazenly boiled down to 'asks Herman Rogers for a child', and Morton writes that this bizarre request 'seemingly' took place a few days before her wedding (which in his lumpen style he calls 'the big day') to the duke. He omits to mention that Wallis was then already in her early forties.

All the old saws are dragged up, such as the sexual tricks she's said to have learned in Shanghai brothels. But in the 1920s it was par for the course for western women to visit such places, with opium, sing-song girls and strange oriental techniques on tap; the madam of one would demonstrate the Cleopatra Clip, which Morton writes – without hint of irony – could have taught Wallis 'to pick up a sovereign'.

Morton prints reams of sour remarks by people who only just, or never, met her, and gives special attention to those who held a grudge. Strangely, as I was writing this, a friend texted that the Queen Mother once told her: 'I think I ought to write down that I didn't hate the Duchess of Windsor. You can't hate someone you don't know.'

It's only fair to say her equanimity was not reciprocated by Wallis; but the few remaining who knew her, myself included, found her sympathetic, affectionate and unpretentious, as well as enormous fun. Morton repeats, yet again, instances of her stern treatment of the Duke — but surely all couples have some rows during a marriage as long as theirs. If she did have an affair, I'm told it was with the star of a long-running Broadway musical who is still alive, and has never uttered a word.

Handed his Diana book on a plate, Morton is clearly out of his depth here. He has simply employed researchers to dig for new dross, to which he's bolted on peripheral names to dress his assertions with spurious authenticity: and to give his ploddingly banal style an intellectual gloss he even quotes Hegel, for God's sake.

Wallis Windsor's difficult role and the great dignity she brought to it deserve re-evaluating. Someone soon will do so. Meanwhile, what she doesn't deserve is Andrew Morton.

THE REAL LEE RADZIWILL

The New York Times Style Magazine

'Oo-h. You're here already!' The voice, lively, with its unmistakable husky drop, comes in to the living room. I turn from the balcony that looks out onto the Avenue Montaigne.

'Oo-h' – again, that low last note – 'how did you get here so quickly?'

Framed in the evening light, between double doors, is a figure slight as swan's-down, a silhouette in dark, skinny Armani pants and a silk T-shirt. The hair, cut for over half a century by the experts on two, at least, continents, is now a sleek chignon, blond, perhaps, with the light around it, darker as she moves toward me. I explain that the Eurostar now has a service where you order a taxi on the train and, hey, presto! At the Gare du Nord, there is a driver, bearing your name.

'Really? I didn't know that. I must go to London more often. I know, I should, but I am so, so happy in this apartment . . . if I can wade through the scores of Japanese kids fighting their way into Chanel.'

The haunting voice and the almost ethereal figure are Lee Radziwill's, and they have been a lifelong part of her enduring identity. But those characteristics are not nearly the whole picture. I am confronted by a subtly strong presence and personality, part wreathed in the glamour of the past, part intensely modern in outlook

and awareness. Not for her any all-too-easy reminis-
cences of 'those days'. She is, quite clearly, herself.

In a world of passing celebrity, Lee Radziwill, sev-
enty-nine, possesses a timeless aura that radiates now-
ness. Her bang up-to-date personal style, her laid-back
– to say pared down would be to demean its ordered
luxury – apartment in Paris ('the favorite of any home
I've ever had'), in this, her favored city, shows how
subtly she has lived, lives now, without the attendant
glare of past pomp and present self-glorification that
others crave. She is utterly content, and it shows. What
she is not is casual. She regulates her life by standards
inbuilt by experience, by nurturing her friendships, by
staying true, by her irony, by her humor, all qualities
that show she is the real deal. That past sorrows and
joys have merged into an elegance that permeates
her presence, that 'something in the air' that indicates
class and courage and composure. Though she now
rigorously guards her privacy, her free spirit surfaces
easily, and her thoughts come crystal clear. A figure of
her time, our history, Lee is her own harbinger for an
iconic future. Ours, and hers.

One sees why Lee is happy. The apartment, just high
up enough to encompass most of the most famous
Parisian landmarks, low enough to allow her to sometimes use the stairs to walk Zinnia, a wriggling bundle
of snow-white fur, is tailor-made for her lifestyle. The
living room, a symphony of light and white and the
deep pink of falling rose petals. Around the fireplace,
a banquette and armless chairs, covered with crisp
white linen printed with tumbling Asian figures ('they
go everywhere with me, every house, my apartment in

New York, my little men') and against the far wall, a sofa of luscious rose silk, thick and ribbed, its back a relaxed baroque scroll. The art on the walls is mostly contemporary, mostly monochrome, most signed, all highly personal. The flowers, two low glass cylinders, a massed spectrum of pinks and reds ('the man who does them for Dior brings them') fill the Parisian dusk with their heady scent.

'Come sit', Lee says, folding her legs into the sofa's cushioned recesses. 'Some vodka?' 'Sure!' (Over her shoulder to an unseen presence, *Seulement de l'eau plate pour moi.*') Near her is a photograph, recently discovered, sent to her: Lee in a column of brilliant red taffeta couture, at the height of her astonishing beauty. She has no recollection of where it was taken or when.

'Were you always aware of your beauty?'

'From the word go,' she answers simply and honestly. 'But no one else was, then. My mother endlessly told me I was too fat, that I wasn't a patch on my sister. It wasn't much fun growing up with her and her almost irrational social climbing in that huge house of my dull stepfather Hughdie Auchincloss in Washington. I longed to be back in East Hampton, running along the beaches, through the dunes and the miles of potato fields my father's family had owned. And even in summer, when we'd go to Hammersmith Farm . . . the Auchincloss place in Newport, a house more Victorian or stranger you can't imagine . . . it wasn't much better. Well, at least there was the ocean, but naturally my sister claimed the room overlooking Narragansett Bay, where all the boats passed out. All I could see from my window was the cows named Caroline and Jacqueline.

(My real first name is Caroline.) Oh, I longed to go back, to be with my father. He was a wonderful man, you'd have loved him. He had such funny idiosyncrasies, like always wearing his black patent evening shoes with his swimming trunks. One thing which infuriates me is how he's always labeled the drunk black prince. He was never drunk with me, though I'm sure he sometimes drank, due to my mother's constant nagging. You would, and I would. The only time I ever saw him really drunk was at Jackie's wedding. He was to give her away, but my mother refused to let him come to the family dinner the night before. So he went to his hotel and drank from misery and loneliness. It was clear in the morning that he was in no state to do anything, and I remember my mother screaming with joy, 'Hughdie, Hughdie, now you can't give Jackie away.' During the wedding party I had to get him onto a plane back to New York. Accompanied by my first husband, also drunk. It was a nightmare.

But we were talking about the Hamptons. It was so empty then, houses miles apart. We lived fairly near my aunt Edie Beale and I'd play with her daughter, Little Edie, even though she was quite a bit older. Grey Gardens was a beautiful house, but I lost touch when I married and lived in England. Later, I had my own house in East Hampton, and went to visit them, with Peter Beard. My God, you should have seen the place! And them! But they were sweet and funny and happily living in their own world. The original idea for the film was to be about my return to East Hampton after thirty years and to have my aunt Edith narrate my nostalgia and hers. So we phoned the Maysles brothers. Initially

the Edies were against it, but the Maysles charmed
them as they only worked with sixteen-millimeter cameras, and we were finally allowed in. . . . The remake is
good. Have you seen it? . . . Listen, I booked a table at
Voltaire. We should leave at . . . what? . . . 8:15. Is that
O.K.?'

The taxi swings into the Place de la Concorde. 'You
know, Paris, well, at least this part of it, has hardly
changed since Jackie and I first came here in 1951.
We were so young! It was the first time we felt really
close, carefree together, high on the sheer joy of getting
away from our mother; the deadly dinner parties of
political bores, the Sunday lunches for the same people
that lasted hours, Jackie and I not allowed to say a
word. Not that we wanted to, except to a lovely man
called James Forrestal, our secretary of defense, who
had a bit of the culture we craved. Jackie's dream was
France, but mine was really art and Italy, as that was all
I cared about through school. My history of art teacher,
who saved my life at Farmington, was obsessed with
Bernard Berenson and I succumbed as well. My first
discovery of him was when we were taken to visit the
Isabella Stewart Gardner Museum, better known then
as Fenway Court. Berenson had chosen all the most
important paintings Isabella should buy. I had another
life open.

'I wrote to Berenson at I Tatti, several letters; then
out of the blue he replied, asking me to come and see
him if I ever came to Italy. Well, that was it. I thought of
nothing else. So after we were here, I went to Florence.
Florence and Berenson and I Tatti! Imagine! Any artistic intellect I possess is due to that time. He took me

under his wing, read to me, encouraged me to write. In fact he published a letter I wrote him. That was my proudest moment. I went back to I Tatti last summer. Though there was no B.B., and no Nicky Mariano, the atmosphere is still the same, though now there are maybe a hundred people there, great scholars-to-be of Renaissance art studying, learning, in those almost monk-like surroundings, eating at a beautiful long oak table. He was one of the most fascinating men I ever knew.'

The doorman opens the taxi door.

'Bonsoir, Princesse.'

We go inside.

'Madame!'

'Madame la Princesse!'

'Princesse Radziwill, je suis ravi de vous voir!'

This fabulous ancien régime politeness to Lee, who has booked the table, and the taxi, and my hotel room, as Mme. Radziwill. One sees why she likes Paris.

'Believe me, when I used to come here with Nureyev or Lenny Bernstein, there was none of that. I was a pimple beside their stature and genius. When I was young, I used to think that everyone should die at seventy . . . but my closest friends, like Rudolf and Andy [Warhol] and to an extent Capote, let alone most of my close family . . . didn't even reach that age. There is something to be said for being older, and memories. How could I ever forget Rudolf's funeral, here, at the Opera . . . the whole place swathed with deep red roses, and draped in black, as well as the dancers and les petits rats descending the stairs. I've seen some extraordinary funerals in my life, Jack's of course. That had a different kind of sadness, a bleak, brutal, tragic end to hopes for a greater future and the buoyant few years of his presidency . . . the opening up of the White House to artists and musicians; I can't deny those few years were glamorous, being on the presidential yacht for the America's Cup races, the parties with the White House en fête. It was so ravishing. People think it was decorated by Sister Parish . . . well, a bit was . . . but really it was Stéphane Boudin of Jansen, who Jackie had met here in Paris; and, as well, Jack's charismatic charm and enthusiasm for life. I remember the first time Jackie asked Jack to Merrywood, to pick her up for some dinner. You couldn't mention the word — 'Democrat' in my stepfather's house or even presence — nor in my father's for that matter — and I felt Jack was in for a rough ride. But he was a senator, so he already had a kind of authority as well as a dazzling personality. He won them over pretty quickly.

My life could certainly have been different. Not so much because Jackie married a Kennedy, but because he became president. If he'd lost the election, I'd have probably spent most of my life in England with Stas, whom I adored, as did anyone who knew him, and our children, Anthony and Tina. We had this divine house on Buckingham Place behind the palace, and the prettiest country place in Oxfordshire . . . Turville Grange . . . that Mongiardino decorated. He glued the walls of the dining room with Sicilian scarves, and asked Lila di Nobili to paint each child with their favorite animals crisscrossed by bands of flowers. It was enchanting. Sadly Lila lacquered over them, so I couldn't take them when we left. To me, that's the essence of great design. It was a perfect Turgenev room . . . something simple and original that stays in the mind forever. Like I Tatti, and Nancy Lancaster's Ditchley Park. Or Peter Beard's house in Montauk. But I wasn't always so pure in my taste. As a child, the person I admired most in the world was Lana Turner! She seemed the epitome of glamour, and her glitzy surroundings so enviable, the opposite of my mother's extremely banal taste. And of course no one had as much taste as Rudolf, vast 19th-century paintings of naked men on glowing velvet walls, Russian-Oriental fabrics and furs, all on a huge scale. He was so impressed with what Mongiardino did for me that he took him for himself and some of his ballets.

We weren't taught anything like that as children. In fact, my childhood taught me nothing . . . zero. I never saw a play with my mother until I was fourteen and then it was 'Hansel and Gretel.' My father, naturally, spoiled me when I was allowed to see him — flying to New York from Washington, alone, in those terrifying planes. He'd take me to Danny Kaye movies and rent a dog for me to walk in the park on Sunday — a different dog every Sunday — and then to have butterscotch sundaes with almonds at Schrafft's. My mother simply had me, sticking me with a series of horrible governesses. There was one particular beast called Aggie, who I remember well. I hadn't a clue how to be a parent myself, and I expect I put Tina and Anthony through tough times. I find it hard to read people's minds, my own children's minds even harder. But it all worked out and I was blessed with two wonderful children. Anthony and I were wonderfully close in the years before he died, and my daughter, Tina, who leads the most original life, is coming to stay with me in Italy soon for four weeks. . . . I say, it's awfully late, you must be exhausted and I know I am.'

It's late in the evening and the apartment is dark now, with only a pool of silvery-pink light on the sofa as Lee walks me to the door, Zinnia bouncing between our feet.

'No, Zinny! Tomorrow! And you, too, tomorrow . . . let's have breakfast at L'Avenue in the sunshine. Good night!' The door gently shuts, the elevator opens. All so easy, so civilized.

One can see why she likes Paris.

Half awake, I lie collecting thoughts, the bare facts, of the near-legend I have just left . . . Caroline Lee Bouvier . . . born in 1933 to John V. Bouvier III and Janet Lee, four years after her sister Jacqueline. Becomes stepdaughter of Hugh D. Auchincloss Jr.

Married:

1) 1953, Michael Canfield.

2) 1959, Prince Stanislas 'Stas' Radziwill; two children, Anthony and Christina ('Tina').

3) 1988, Herbert Ross, film director.

Lives in the United States and France.

The lesser-known facts are the fodder of tabloids. Her duplicitous treatment by the whims of Aristotle Onassis. Her great friend Truman Capote, insisting Lee should act, adapts 'Laura' as a vehicle for her, but stage fright prevents her from pursuing a theatrical career. Her romances with the most attractive men of the time — the photographer Peter Beard and Richard Meier, the architect, possibly even Mick Jagger, among them. The last-minute calling off of her wedding to the San Francisco hotelier Newton Cope. Unfulfilling years, exacerbated by her sister's escalating ill health, their difficult relationship and a certain amount of friction with her children, led Lee to bouts of deep depression and occasional dips into alcoholism, both bravely, the latter publicly, divulged and eradicated. Indeed, so much so that she was able to cope, resiliently, with the death of her nephew John F. Kennedy Jr., to whom she was extremely close, followed, shockingly soon after, by that of her son, Anthony, from a rare form of cancer.

These tragedies, compounded by earlier, unforgettably tragic memories, convinced Lee to make, if not a new life, a different one: one where the press is gentler; where her past, good or infamous, is not daily revisited; and where she can be surrounded by so many of the things she grew up with and learned to love about Europe. In 1974 she and Jackie published *One Special Summer*, a memoir of their European trip, written originally as a gift to their parents, and in 2001 Lee wrote a second memoir, *Happy Times*, published by her friends, the Assoulines. It's an engaging picture of some of the most glorious moments in her vivid life. She says the best part was being hands-on in its production, discussing the layout, the typefaces, selecting photographs from among myriad images.

We meet, as she said we would, in the sunshine, at the chic cafe spitting distance from her building. Chairs are arranged for her, water, espresso and an ashtray brought without a word said.

'Well?' she says, 'what's next?'

'Tell me about your marriages.'

'Oh.' Short now, taken aback, no low note and a long pause. 'O.K., where shall we start?' I say, 'The first?' Another pause. 'Michael Canfield? O.K. . . . I was very young when we met, and he was so good-looking and clever. I wanted so badly to get away from my mother, and he seemed to offer everything . . . looks, privilege, friends, fun. His father was chairman of Harper & Brothers, so he led a very literary life and was a brilliant editor. I was deliriously happy for a while, moving to London, our house in Chester Square . . . but . . . he drank seriously. He was very fragile. One day I couldn't open the front door, he was slumped, out cold, inside. He tried to stop, but nothing worked for any time. He said I was so in tune with life and he wasn't any longer. And besides, I had met Stas . . . Stas was divorcing at the time, and we fell in love and eventually we married. . . . Those were glorious years. Being married to Stas was certainly the happiest part of my life, so he must have been the love of my life: there were other infatuations, other loves even, but never the joy or knowledge of life and living that I experienced with Stas. . . . Jack and my sister would come over, staying in Buckingham Place rather than the embassy, and I'd be included in all the great events, dinners at Buckingham Palace, you know. And the trip to India. The best part of that was meeting Nehru, he was seductive, mentally rather than physically, not unlike Berenson, and so beautiful, and with the most exquisite soft golden skin. We stayed in his house and he showed us to our rooms every night, showing us the books we should read, which made one feel completely at home.

Stas and I went to Washington often . . . and then.

. . .' Her voice trails off as she stares into the sun, perhaps considering the end of her marriage to Stas. 'More
coffee?' 'Well, there was Jack's death and . . . and . . .
Ari. Listen, I think the world knows more about all that
than I do. He was dynamic, irrational, cruel I suppose,
but fascinating. He also had the most beautiful skin,
and smelled wonderful. Naturally, I mean. Fascinating .
. . as my sister discovered!'

'And Herbert Ross?'

'Oh no, do we have to talk about that? O.K., he was
certainly different from anybody else I'd been involved
with, and the film world sounded exciting. Well, it
wasn't. I hated Hollywood, and the provincialism of
the industry. . . Herbert had been married to the balle-
rina Nora Kaye until she died, and unbeknownst to me
was still obsessed by her. It was "Nora said this, Nora
did it like that, Nora liked brown and orange." . . . If
anybody even breathed her name, Herbert would burst
into tears. I had to clench my fists every time and was
deeply hurt as I thought I had created a wonderful
life for him. Thank God we never really settled in Los
Angeles. My New York was difficult for Herbert, so we
parted. . . . Now, no more on husbands!'

'Then let's go back to the president's assassination,' I
say. 'Do you remember where you were?'

Lee pauses. 'As if yesterday. It was in the evening,
in London. Stas came running up the stairs, his voice
and face in shock. I started crying . . . uncontrollably.
For hours. Finally he said, 'Lee, you have to get ahold
of yourself', and I stopped, suddenly. It was the last
time I have ever cried. I've never cried since, never.
Anthony's death was equally soul destroying, but with

an illness it's so distressing . . . coupled with his bravery throughout it. I could only cry inner tears. When he died, I was already cried out. And I certainly wouldn't cry about myself, or my life. In some funny way I'm lucky that there was so much more interest in my sister. Which, of course, I understand. I enjoy reading about real celebrities even now, and Jackie certainly qualified in that league. Of course, when you are closely related to someone so in the public eye, you tend to think the interest is dumb or trivial because you know the person, and the truth. But I certainly understand peoples' fascination. After all, as the young wife of the youngest elected president, she was fascinating.

As to that interest in her spilling over into my life? Well, at times it was annoying, at times funny. Perhaps the most depressing part was that whatever I did, or tried to do, got disproportionate coverage purely because of Jackie being my sister. But you learn to deal with the scrutiny, even the lies, as long as it's not malicious.

Regrets? I think everyone has regrets, and people who say they haven't are either liars . . . or narcissists. There have been many things in my life to have regrets about, in the sense I wish I could have changed them, or somehow made them not happen. What I don't have is envy. I'm perfectly content at this time of my life. I've done so many fascinating things and the greatest joy is that I continue to do interesting things and meet fascinating people. Working for Diana Vreeland at Harper's Bazaar was a great learning curve. Working in P.R. for Giorgio Armani taught me a lot about that particular —I almost said 'peculiar' – industry. And I met my dearest friend, Hamilton South, while there.

Really, the most fulfilling roles have been my friendships , Berenson, Nureyev, Peter, even Andy Warhol because he was so wildly different — then, and now Bernard-Henri Lévy and his wife, Arielle Dombasle, and Giambattista Valli, and Diego Della Valle, who are all angelic to me.

Am I melancholy by nature? Less so, now, and I certainly don't bounce out to parties and talk all night. One can't help but be a bit melancholy when you see how the world has changed, and I don't mean that nostalgically. Every day one is confronted by words and visions of human misery. You would have to have a heart of ice not to be a bit melancholy. I've been happy, and am happy now. My life has been exciting, active, changeable. At my age, one is lucky to have old friends, and, fortunately, most of them, like me, can't seriously work a computer and the phone is our link. So I'm not lonely. I have this apartment, this view, my bursting-with-light New York apartment . . . yes, and you, Zinny . . . this *douceur de vivre*, this city.'

One can see why Paris loves Lee.

BRYANT'S TYRANTS

The Spectator

A review of *Entitled: A Critical History of the British Aristocracy* by Chris Bryant

I rashly discarded this book's dust jacket when I received it, and thus saw only the unlettered cover, a faded photograph of three generations of an aristocratic family, somewhat camera-shy in their silken breeches. Oh I see, I thought, this is one of those books on the foibles of the aristocracy, always an entertaining subject.

How wrong can one be? Instead, it's a polemic against crats aristo, auto, mono or pluto; and the author apparently yearns for any crat of a different stripe — not just demo and bureau, but mobo, neo and probably ochlo to boot. Naturally I went immediately to the index, to look up my family. It lists just one member, Eric, 10th Earl of Bessborough, who, as Chris Bryant somewhat sarkily puts it, had an 'enthusiasm for the stage' — a harmless and rather pantisocratic pursuit one might think.

But of course there's nothing about Eric's more substantial forebears, among them the 2nd Earl, an important and admired ambassador to the Sublime Porte; or the 9th, a memorable 20th-century governor general of Canada; let alone the several Ponsonbys who were influential Whig politicians in Ireland; or Sir Fritz and Sir Henry, father and son, between them private secretary to the monarch from Queen Victoria to George V.

Bryant's theory is that anyone who ever held the crown, power, wealth or position in Britain was a land-grabbing, money-grubbing, rubbing-under-lings-noses-in-their-poverty tyrant. And not just your run-of-the-mill Richards and Henrys and Georges. No, no; he starts around the year 700, when surely things were a mite less civilised than they became, and we wade through several chapters on Sigered of Essex and Cenewuf of Mercia, earldormen Odda, Aethelnoth and Oslac and their various wapentake sons, Aelfgar, Wulfheah, Ufegeat and Yffrunts. They are mirthless names to conjure lucidity from, though dear old King Canute (spelt Cnut) is good for a laugh each time he turns up.

Nobles, like most other people, were murdered or died of disease, childbirth or in battle by about the age of 35, so hastily bestowed titles change hands every few pages here: young Warwicks become Hertford or Arundel or Suffolk with mystifying frequency. Each one is portrayed as a more power-crazed brute than the last (though now and again the author lets his class-bashing mask slip, when they're described as 'from an illustrious family'). Never is there any suggestion that the less well-born might indulge in even the mildest form of fisticuffs or corruption.

The Middle Ages are all blood and bloody-minded-ness, these tyrants 'littering' castles all over the land, which at least must have given their 'thegns' something to do, even at a minuscule wage, though how many would have been employed building and furnishing exquisite cathedrals and chapels is never contemplated. Just the opposite: in the mid-16th century, Robert Earl of Salisbury's 'reckless mania' in spending £39,000 on an elaborate garden — with a 'water feature' embellished with artificial shells, fish and snakes — gets Bryant's anti-beauty dander up. He also blames the tradition of horse breeding and racing on the aristocracy, which would have come as news to gypsies, and to a populace for whom, before football, races were the main source of recreation.

Many noblemen were deeply religious, and raised massive armies with which to crusade, rightly or wrongly, through seethingly hostile lands to Jerusalem, though such bravura doesn't stir the author's bloodless heart. Perhaps he should ponder this: without such men's faith, had Suleiman conquered Vienna in 1529, within a few decades all of Europe might have become Muslim.

Being constantly bludgeoned with reminders of past sins only serves to set people against one another. I met a high-ranking Indian diplomat recently who said he wished the British press would stop banging on about Partition: 'We don't even think about it, it's done, over.' This book has the same determination to exacerbate old wounds, even though the Marxist life-style it advocates was barely a gleam in that Hampstead hero's eye by the time we get to the last two chapters. It's hard to believe that all our countrymen have been serially vicious in one echelon and utterly downtrodden in the others.

Back to that cover. It's the Pembroke family, and I

knew the youngest pictured, one of the gentlest of men, given to quiet good works. His son was a film-maker, and his grandson's role in life is to repair and improve the ravishing house built by their forebears, as it is with many other families. There are now very few brutal or rapacious 'nobles' of the grim persuasion described in this book. That baton has been taken up by a different slew of our compatriots.

ROMANA MCEWEN

An Appreciation

Romana McEwen, who died recently, enhanced the lives of all who knew her. As the wife of the musician and artist Rory McEwen ('the finest botanical painter since and including Redoute') whose testimonial exhibition at Kew Gardens in 2013 she was deeply instrumental in arranging, her houses in both London and Scotland were centres of social , intellectual and artistic circles following her marriage in 1958. Film-makers, wits, poets and painters and the many talented members of Rory's family flocked through her ever-open door into rooms hung with early works by Bacon, Hockney, Twombly, Dine and Brigid Riley; while Roman's four children, each currently practitioners of this cultural inheritance, sat spellbound at the crossed-legged figure of Ravi Shankar as he played his newest raga.

Romana's ability to create so essentially English an atmosphere is all the more extraordinarily given her lineage. Her mother's father, the New York magnate John Jacob Astor, had drowned on the Titanic leaving his daughter Alice not only a substantial fortune, bit also acknowledged American Indian, and possibly Cuban, blood. Anglophile to her fine-limbed fingertips – 'Alice's wrists began at her elbows' as Cecil Beaton would later write – she bought Hanover Lodge in Regent's Park, which became a nucleus for the literary and artistic members of inter-war society.

Among these was Raimund, the exuberant son of Hugo von Hofmannsthal, Austria's world-acclaimed poet and librettist of many Richard Strauss' operas, most famously Der Rosenkavalier. Following their marriage, and Romana's birth in 1935, Alice and Raimund summered at their baroque home, Schloss Kammer on the Attersee in Austria. The idyll was shattered one evening during a dinner party on the lake. Suddenly there were fireworks on the darkening mountainside: 'Oh Raimund, how magical!' guests exclaimed. 'But I didn't arrange fireworks' Raimund answered. They watched in horror as it became clear the 'fireworks' were a vast burning swastika. Forthwith, packing up the hose (the cases remained totally unscathed on Dover docks for the duration on the ensuing war), Alice, taking Romana, sailed for New York where she was brought up by her beloved governess, Dermy; and it was there, twenty-odd years later, that she met Rory McEwen, and with him, returned to settle in this country for the rest of her life.

Romana's exquisite manners, inherited from both her parents, her supremely unpretentious style of living, her generosity, her vivacity and gurgling laugh, her beauty and spirit, in which the varied skeins of her ancestry were frequently discernable, will be treasured by all who knew her. Among the tangible treasures she leaves are her own landscape paintings: always watercolour, always small, always finely detailed and executed, but with a wonderfully dotty sense of scale. Animals...especially cats...sit oversize in intricate gardens, beloved dogs dwarf a snowy Alpine landscape. In art, as in life, Romana McEwen gave heart and humour to the legions who loved her, and to the surroundings she so meticulously created.

I ONCE MET MARTIN LUTHER KING

The Oldie

When writing for such erudite publications as this, it's always wise to try to strip the prose to the bone, not employ too many (if any) adjectives and names, or face the fury of editors wielding their red pens. On the other hand, when I perform my cabaret, I am always encouraged to add more anecdotes between the songs as 'people love them', I'm sure the former is the correct formula, but I'm forced to say the latter applies in this case. What follows happened over fifty years ago, but if the details are somewhat hazy, the cast of characters involved in that unforgettable occasion remain clear as daylight:

It's an early Spring evening in New York, in 1963. America is at the height of the euphoria of the Kennedy administration, and if most eyes are on the golden-boy president, there are the tarnishments of his Attorney General brother's alleged – then – affair with Marilyn, the now-dead dream-girl for whom, six months earlier, I'd been selected, by my boss at Vogue, to show her the contacts of a secret, near-naked sitting: her last. More disturbingly, there's the ever-rising rumble of disquiet in the South, where Governor George Wallace of Alabama is scarcely more than a month away from his speech expounding 'segregation forever'.

Meanwhile, Central Park has turned green, as it

always does, overnight: the fountains are playing outside the Plaza, the late papers have photographs of
Jackie leaving Le Club in her newest Oleg Cassini. I
walk from my apartment on 77th and Madison across
to Lena Horne's on Amsterdam Avenue.

Lena, the sublimely talented singer and actress, and
possibly the most beautiful woman I ever saw, has
asked me to go with her to a concert arranged by Frank
Sinatra to boost the singing career of his son Frank Jr
– in my blurred memory to take place in Carnegie Hall,
though more probably it was somewhere slightly less
classical, nearby – and Lena has gathered some of her
now-legendary musician friends to encourage young
Blue Eyes.

So I drink Old Fashioneds with Duke Ellington,
and his brilliant shadow Billy Strayhorn, among others, while Lena tells of a recent humiliating experience
involving a hotel in one of the Southern states, though
how anyone could not want this icon of sophisticated
elegance on their premises is incomprehensible. Then
we Carey Car across town to the venue. Frank Jr. sings
pretty well, but his dad has clearly had a few. At the
party onstage afterwards he sways up to Lena and says
something that makes her pull abruptly away. As she
turns back, I see a tear on her cheek. Then suddenly,
out of the smoky blue, there are the shining white teeth
and wide, black smile of Louis Armstrong, who com-
forts Lena in enfolding arms.

Composed now, she waves across the room and in a
moment, at our sides, are standing Martin Luther King
and his wife Coretta. She is wearing demure white lace,
and through it I can, even now, see the delicate bronze

of the skin on her arms as we shake hands...both hers and Dr King's have that faint purplish sheen, as smooth and glowing as the rarest Cuban mahogany, and they are both so vibrantly alive. I hear the deep, gentle tone of his voice as we talk, and fix my eyes on the profile that had recently come to auger, along with JFK's humaneness, a new, enlightened dawn.

Within months, that humanity was blown to bits, in Texas, and within half a decade, the vibrant eyes and gentle voice, though fiercer now, in Mississippi. And the gilded towers of that new Camelot crumbled, but the ramparts of Dr King's dream castle were rising.

LUCY BIRLEY

An Eulogy

I read, somewhere, that the Plantation owners in the Deep South used to have wire cages, filled with fire-flies, hung in the branches of the magnolia trees, silver-grey with Spanish moss, to light the path of evening guests through the Bayou to those white-columned porticos.

I think of Lucy as having an incandescence, like these romantic creatures........glittering, darting, momentarily invisible, now glowing, now a transient amber spark trailing a hum of murmured laughter, to hover in star-sprinkled darkness...... Lucy, above all, had an affinity with nature, and these dancing, fugitive, fireflies seem to symbolize her own, rare, essence.

Thus it is perhaps appropriate that the most famous of those Southern mansions is George Washington's Mount Vernon, so-named by that exemplary President's ancestors after a remote village on Ireland's most Western coast, and it was here that Lucy was largely raised. Here, where ageless, smoothed rocks lie in strange slabs beside the violent ocean, and wind-bent woods give scant shelter, her childhood formed that affinity, one she has passed on to her four sons, particularly to Otis, my godson, and to Isaac, to Tara, whom I was partly instrumental in naming, and Merlin...... Could Lucy, perhaps, have chosen to remain there, roaming, caring for a wounded bird or injured hare, riding rough ponies to distant cliff-tops? Certainly, she would return again and again to this tousled landscape of her youth.

But there was, as well, something more *mondain* in Lucy's make-up.......an innate chic, and beauty to go with it. Quick to learn, and blessed with a subtle sense of humour, the wildness blossomed into the sleek sophisticate we are all here today, filled with gratitude and love tinged by sorrow, to commemorate; and each with our own special memories of Lucy's often quixotic, but always enchanting, persona. A persona that lit our lives as brightly as those fireflies.

With the sophistication came elegance ...*'languid, loungy elegance'* as her close friend Tom Bell describes it...and a kind of insouciance, not to say impudence.... a combination that conspired to captivate Bryan. Together, flying high and adored, feted by the famous and photographed by the finest, Lucy's idiosyncratic visual impact was in perfect rapport with Bryan's matchless style and finely-honed taste.....Their boys came rapidly, so close in age to play like kittens and fight like cats...... seeming, as Harriet Vyner, Lucy's friend from teenage years, astutely puts it, *'worldly and wild, like children in a story by Saki'*. And that *enfilade* of ravishing, music-filled rooms at Little Bognor, with Bryan's unerring eye for the arts, was the catalyst for their formative years.

Lucy also believed childhood should have this wide freedom, especially if that freedom included her.....*'Mum was always one of us'* was the theme, and on spurs of the moment she took them to famed

or infallible friends in foreign places. To filmmaker
Amanda Eliasch with Tara in Provence, to Paris, where,
one stormy night, Rupert Everett watched as her dress
swirled round her; *'pure Salome, darling'*......and
to early Prince gigs:...... to Los Angeles where, Anne
Lambton recalls, *'Lucy promised they could each choose
a book at Borders. Merlin, all of about eight, showed
me his choice. "LUCY!!!, I shrieked....LOOK!!!" "Well, I
DID promise" said Lucy airily......followed by that deep,
unexpected, belly laugh....Merlin had chosen 'How to
Be a Successful Lesbian' "...'*

Lucy had a sentimental, if tenuous, grasp on tech-
nology. Taking them to stay with Jasper and Camilla
Guinness in Tuscany, she'd rented a fancy, gleaming,
Alfa Romeo automatic. Foot down, thrilled at the roar
of the powerful engine, she shouted *'Isn't it amazing....
sounds just like an aeroplane'*. After some time on the
motorway, Isaac surreptitiously slid the gear stick from
grinding Low to noiseless Drive. *'Don't! she said, I like
it sounding like an aeroplane'*........and she expected
even airlines to fall in with her standards. She stormed
off one – first-class, it goes without saying – flight,
when told to remove her headscarf; another because
she couldn't sit next to Robin........both utterly understandable reasons, it seems to me.

And, of course, she took them back, often, to Mount
Vernon, to her roots, to that wildness, encouraging Otis
to adopt a jackdaw fledgling. Jock became his boon
companion, with Lucy smuggling Jock in her bag
through customs; a kind of danger – cocking a reckless
snoop at petty authority – she reveled in.

Indeed, she, and the entire family once experienced

true danger when a crazed hijacker caused the plane they were on to fall, not once but nerve-shatteringly twice, thousands of feet, and twice almost hitting the ground. The moment the plane stabilized, Lucy did the only sensible thing...lit up a Marlboro Light.

These, and many other examples, show both her capriciousness and her fortitude. Rules might be there to be broken, or more often ignored....she was a fearless queue-barger....but there was one that even her boys learned to respect. Otis once mildly told her '*Mum, you can't just go buying horses all over the place*'. Lucy whipped round...'*Don't you EVER tell me what I can or can't do*'.

And herein perhaps lies the core of her character. Her abiding belief in individuality.... (her own most certainly included).... and an intrinsic inclination not to tell others what to do. This could be interpreted as a somewhat lax approach to life, but there are many instances when selflessness spurred sheer kindness... witness, as Catherine Hesketh noted, her instantly flying to South Africa to tend and bring home her desperately sick, beloved neighbor, Nicky Lane. And as Sophia Stewart maintains, Lucy's loyalty had no boundaries.

But if no-one could tell Lucy what to do, she was doing a lot herself. She wrote, along with poetry... maybe even, as she told Amanda Harlech, a novel... and many articles for The Insider on couture – the subject in which she was eminently qualified – while simultaneously making, and exhibiting, her distinctive, highly original photographs. And at home in Shropshire, while attempting to do – somewhat haphazardly, it must be said – domestic things like cooking ... (Harriet remembers her retrieving from the bowels of a sofa, and de-dog-hairing, the roast for dinner)....her energy was, *au fond*, focused on those dogs, her horses, her lambs and hens.... and, paramount, on her children.

With Robin, she became more involved in a gaudier world, flying to parties with presidents, vacations with zillionaires, dinners with....quite possibly.... dictators. But the being-bored threshold wasn't left at any butler-ed door. During one fearfully swell event in Washington, she fainted dead away. Security goons 911'd their 'phones, an ambulance was summoned, stretcher-men carried the limp body to its doors. Then Lucy nipped blithely up its steps, hissing to Robin *'I couldn't stand the boredom ONE MINUTE LONGER'.*

If Hertford Street brought with it a more urban environment, her instinct for putting people together added much éclat to the club's planned, and now fabled, glamour. It was Lucy who, loving Rifat Ozbek's phenomenal taste, introduced him to Robin... *'Without Lucy, there'd be no Loulou's'*, Rifat says.

Robin's inherited Birley poise and pursuit of excellence jived deftly with Lucy's more *outré* aesthetic. She was a vivacious hostess with Robin, though, while happily basking in being the boss's wife, she sometimes found city etiquette confining, and was not averse to an unsubtly-voiced *critique* of patrons she thought didn't pass muster.

Almost my last visual memory of Lucy is sitting with her, smoking, on that bum-rail by the fire in the outdoor Terrace at Hertford Street. Seeing some slight action she found irritating in someone across the room, she beckoned Michael. *'Have that man thrown out!'*

Michael blanched....'*I don't think that's a very good idea, My Lady. He's the major investor*'. Lucy shrugged conspiratorially, and with a hint of that belly laugh, flicked her cigarette into the fire. Sparks flared.... dancing, glowing, flying up... and away.

Like Lucy....away.....to some distant, star-sprinkled, dome.

BOOKS OF THE YEAR

The Spectator

I don't really care, and I'm sure you don't either, if Duchess Kate agrees to a photoshoot, or whether Dolce and Gabbana will show up at the gala Centenary dinner *at all*, but you will, when you read the magazine's editor Alexandra Shulman, in *'Inside Vogue: A Diary of My Hundredth Year'*. Candidly, introspectively, generously and wittily written, it shows the slog and guts and diplomacy needed to produce the magazine, often to the detriment of family life. The eventual, successful results of this year's long-planned coups de chic are sheer page-turners.

The people of Thierry Coudert's *'The Beautiful People of the* Café *Society'* are surely anything but café – chateau and yacht, more like – in *'Scrapbooks by the Baron de Chabrol'*. Starting in the '30s, Fred de Cabrol painted faux-naif watercolours of the grandest European houses, gardens and resorts, enlivening them with *decoupe* photographs, cuttings, invitations and menus of their frequenters, at balls, races, hunts, weddings, beaches. It's a lavish panoply of a long-forgotten world, revealing the elegant style, decors, and beauties of those pre – and surprisingly, *during* – and post-war years, one of the most serenely elegant being his wife, Daisy who is shown wearing a simple couture creation *'franfruluchee'*, delicious word, with ribbons.

The war doesn't seem to have stopped the de Cabrol set having a gay old time, or Chanel holing up in the Ritz with her Abwehr officer, and other *collaborateuses horizontale*, but Anne Sebba, in her almost audibly-written and meticulously-researched *'Les Parisiennes'*, paints a very different picture or the many other women who witnessed, watched and worked against the humiliation and terror the Nazi occupiers inflicted on that city, and to preserve some vestige of dignity and continuity in the years of almost total deprivation. Not too many ribbons during this time; rather more Ribbentrop, and his like.

TONGUE SANDWICH

The Spectator

A review of *A Humour of Love:
A Memoir* by Robert Montagu

D on't be misled by the book's title. It is not funny.
That 'Humour' denotes humouring rather than
fun. Anything but. And 'Love'? Well, it takes all
sorts, as they say. This 'affair' delves into that all-too-
current subject, paedophilia.

Robert Montagu's father was Viscount Hinchingbroke.
'Hinch', a much-loved figure in many early 20th C mem-
oirs, soon inherited the (10th) Earldom of Sandwich,
a title (which he was later to renounce) as old as the
Dorset hills surrounding his romantic, grey-gold stone,
Carolingian seat; his upbringing was purely patrician –
Eton, Oxford, the Guards etc. – his career a wool-sack
dyed politician, violently against the Common Market.
Married to the painter Rosemary Peto, Hinch sired sev-
eral children, of which the author was the youngest.

And to him, it was all picture perfect, 'sitting on a
huge lawn...a picnic under the shadow of a cedar tree...
my mother passing the food with the help of a nanny...
Dad wearing a tweed suit, grinning...the older children
spread out across the vast rug...the constant laughter'.
Can't we just see it? And they were perfect, it seems,
those children...one prettier than the other with 'their

wide bone structure and thick, straw-coloured hair'. But none prettier than seven year old Robert.

His father fell in love with him: at first, it seems, behaving like an animal with a cub, licking and stroking and kissing its young: and Robert being happy, each morning, to 'hop into bed and snuggle up to my father's big body in his creamy silk pajamas'. Many children do, or at least used to do, this. It established an unspoken genetic bond, transmitted by odour and voice and touch. But, somewhat unusually, Robert felt a definite attraction to his father's 'big, veined hands, the wide chest and dignified face...I don't feel afraid', even when his pyjama bottoms are gently and sensually pulled off.

'That's better, boyzo. That's so much better', and the father gazes at his child's naked body, a marble faun. An Athenian idyll, he may have thought, initially. But then the kissing had to start...'over every inch of skin, to kiss everything and'...(I tremble to write it)...'to suck'.

Things get hotter with a shared nightly bath. The earl's big, veined hands 'wash my backside, carefully between the cleft...and the foreskin of my penis as he always does'. Tellingly, in the cerebral, questioning rants that follow each incident, the author writes he was 'partly enjoying the experience... odd and wrong, but slightly (sic) delicious'. Eventually that experience penetrates deeper – three inches deeper to be exact – yet strangely these scenes take place, Wagner blasting from Sandwich's wrap-around speaker system, with the bathroom door wide open, and easily visible to any of those flaxen-haired siblings. But they saw, noticed, nor cared a whit, though later, when appraised of their father's mopping-up operations, they chorus, Lady Bracknell-like, 'A handkerchief!'

One feels...and I don't mean condones...a certain sympathy for the father. His beloved young son was, clearly, what we called at Eton, (where he was naturally soon to go, and where he most emphatically was *not*) 'hell's tarty', and, though innocently, a bit of a cock-teaser. Hinch's wife had left him for a woman, his *ancien regime* was collapsing. His perversion – we are told he abused several other boys including, shades of the Wilde trial, the one who delivered the newspapers – was, though we may not like to admit it, not uncommon amongst his generation, as Edward St Aubyn has made us aware. Such filial feelings are known to exist among animals, even ancient civilisations, and love, as *we* know, has infinite humours.

Robert Montagu, now a solidly-married father of four and upstanding founder of the Dorset Child and Family Counseling Trust, wrote this extraordinary 'family' saga long ago, from soon after it started A until the time he left school, and, with Lord Sandwich being dead some years, has just elected to publish it. One can barely believe it really happened; but apart from a few inaccuracies and some youthfully-excusable sloppy syntax, it reads as horribly true. But in the self-and-others-searching passages that follow each narrative section, the author, for all his teenage anger, finally blames no-one, least of all himself.

GIRL POWER

The Spectator

A review of *Full Marks for Trying: An Unlikely Journey from the Raj to the Rag Trade* by Brigid Keenan and *A Girl from Oz* by Lyndall Hobbs.

S ome years ago, working on a project in Tel Aviv, I had a meeting-free weekend. I know, I thought, I'll call my friend Brigid Keenan — at that time *en poste* to Syria with her ambassadorial husband — and nip up to Damascus — so close, only that smidgen of Lebanon in the way. I dialled Brigid's number.

There were many odd whirrs and pings and beeps, and then, 'Don't *ever* call me'. Slam! It was an unexpected reaction from a voice I'm accustomed to hear burble merrily on about how last night their diplomatic reception was brouhaha'd because the dog puked on the First Lady of Baku's shoes, or the joy of discovering a pink sandstone temple half buried in some hidden Kazakhstan valley, or tracking down Marmite in Outer Mongolia. Brigid is rarely at a loss for an anecdote, and never, bar this silenced telephone, for an audience.

I had to wait until we next met for her to explain that the international lines, particularly those from Israel, were, even in those far-off and palmier-seeming days, routinely bugged: but, had I managed to make it to Damascus, I would have been treated to a torrent of the

highly comic and wildly improbable situations this most
practical of diplomats has diffused and delighted in, over
her long career — many of which she has described in
other enchanting books. This, her latest, looks further
back: to her childhood, and to becoming, when barely
in her twenties, the first star of fashion journalism at the
very start of its sudden shoot into The youth quake. It
was a rollercoaster ride with minimal coasting.

Born in India to parents who had long held important positions in the army hierarchy, Brigid grew up
in aya – and syce-staffed residencies during the last
rays of that sullied sunset, though kept unaware of her
father's letters from the Northern Front. These provide,
even now, blood-curdling witness to an empire's death
throes. Uprooted by partition, the Keenans were sum-
marily dismissed from India back to bleak England,
with four children, no pension, no home and penni-
less. Aged relations took them in, in parochial Fleet:
her father found work mucking out on a distant farm,
her mother mucking in with meagre rations of the food,
which to them was 'foreign', a far cry from luscious
mangoes and saffron rice.

Somehow, without hint of grumble, and the sheer
pluck and humour their daughter has inherited in
spades, they turned their life around. Her mother
started a kindergarten and the children excelled at
school and sat in the gods at theatres. Like some twi-
light emblem of a past world, Mrs Keenan arranged for
Brigid to be presented at the last-ever debutante court.
But if parental eyes were looking in the *Gotha,* their
daughter's were gazing longingly at the press — the
Daily Express, to be exact.

That paper, Fleet Street's most avant-garde of its era, was in advance of the still-sluggish changes in postwar attitudes to reporting, realising that youth and young fashion was a seller. Each day, spreads of models in affordably chic dresses appeared, taken by John French, or rather by his stable of assistants —Terry Donovan, Brian Duffy and particularly David Bailey, whose rise coincided with Brigid's innate savviness. Grander newspapers took note, and she was whisked to the *Sunday Times,* quickly becoming the most influential fashion editor of the decade, largely because her pages had an intellectual and humorous approach. Her ability to put voice and image on paper served her then as surely as it does in this book; the wacky trips, the encounters with the famous and infamous, the frights, the disasters, the fun, and all the merry burbling rest — and the rest is her story.

Barely a decade later, Swinging London was to have its boats rocked by another fashion firebrand. Lyndall Hobbs came from even further afield than Brigid, from Melbourne, which, thanks partly to her enchanting looks but more to sheer chutzpah, she had shaken by the scruff of its provincial neck by writing in, and appearing on, her own page in its just-established *Newsday.* She soon followed with a television programme, aged only seventeen.

On a whim and a windfall of £2,000 (yes, still pounds there, then) Lyndall took flight, arriving in London broke-ish but breathtaking. Soon her nous for the newest news made her the youngest female fashion force of the decade. She was groundbreaking (instrumental in getting Dame Edna on stage); rule-breaking (the first person we knew to take a camera to every inner sanctum, including Sandringham) and brow-beating — barging into a Murdoch editor's office. And while too sweet-natured to be a heartbreaker, she certainly stole them away. Michael White, the impresario about to launch the *Rocky Horror Show* on an unsuspecting audience, was her steady throughout these London years. A love-affair with Al Pacino took her to Hollywood, where she still lives, cementing her career as an independent film-maker, as well as being life and breath for Los Angelinos. Her story bubbles with the funny and the famous (and hers are the truly famous), but also reveals less happy periods: her conquering of serious cancer, her long (eventually fulfilled) desire for children, her frequent dashes, half a world away, to care for the father she admired.

As well she might. A trained Spitfire pilot, he was captured by the Japanese almost the day war started. His letters from the south-east Asian front were upbeat: 'Plenty of tennis and fresh air... we're being very well treated' — his family need not despair. Only on his return did he describe the brutal months in Changi prison and the years of slave labour on the Burma railway. In old age, he told Lyndall that not having actually fought was forever on his conscience. That guilt should be assuaged by the courage, vigour and honesty with which his daughter writes this unabashedly artless autobiography.

OBSOLETONIANS

Tatler

We were a fairly uniform lot, the intake to Eton in the first years of the 1950s. Echoes... even visions....of the war shaped our youthful minds. Bomb damage still blighted cities, tattered blackout still flapped on buildings, rationing was still in force. The angular modernity of the Festival of Britain had barely pierced our teen conscience. Perhaps, assimilated from our elders, we hoped against hope the future would return to some version of a not-yet-forgotten past.

So there we were, fresh out of boys school, over-awed by the size and splendour and age of our new surroundings, by a sense of self, of horizons and of space – your own room, from day one – after regimented, dingy confines in sandy Surrey. Now, one might be scared, or lonely, miss Nanny or one's dog, but soon came a visceral challenge: to grapple with emerging adulthood.

We quickly learned the rules....or rather, customs. We dutifully prepared our Saying Lesson before Lights Out, we got up at seven for Early School, went to Absence (in fact, Presence), then Chapel after. We ate revolting Boys Dinner in the allotted 20 minutes before doing battle on the Playing Fields of Sixpenny, or dragged padded grey-flannel shorts down to Boats. We noted the swagger of Sixth Form boys, seemingly wildly grown-up, and were careful to do nothing that might single one out to the gods of Pop. We skeltered to Boy-Calls, we skivvied for Fag-masters, we cleaned their Corps boots, we oiled-up to our Tutors, we flattered our Dames, we 'capped' all Beaks. And we were drunk with relief on graduation from Remove to Upper School.

What all this taught us was to be polite, have good manners, to show respect. Even so vast an institution was essentially intimate: we formed a mutual bond, didn't feel superior, although we scoffed slightly at Tugs, (scholarship boys), jealous of their cleverness rather than from snobbism. This bonding was essential as there was almost no recreation besides sports – except, thank God, the Art Schools. There were no foreigners, though one raven-haired beauty was rumoured to be half-Egyptian…"Crumbs! Egyptian!!" we whispered as he passed. There was no swimming pool, no theatre (concerts, or plays, usually Shakespeare, apt to be desultory affairs in School Hall), no cinema, no medicines (my Dame believed in a scant thimble of brandy cure-all), no cameras or Coca Cola, no radios, TV or gramophones, and most certainly no drinking or smoking – sackable offences, if caught.

These privations weren't exclusively because we were at Eton. There wasn't, *anywhere*, pop music, nor young singing idols (though we knew girls who swooned at Johnny Ray and later jiggled about to Bill Haley), no new humour, no dark Nouvelle Vague films, no Going Abroad – put paid by a £50 currency-limit: the theatre was Anna Neagle comedies, artists were in Paris; night-clubs were for one's parents' friends, smooching to Edmundo Ross; clothes hadn't changed in decades, jeans unheard of. There was no street-life we yearned to emulate (though Teddy-Boys did have a certain allure), no social level to step down to. Drugs were unknown, Du Maurier cork-tips made one dizzy, whiskey in quantity unexpectedly made one sick, putting a sticky end to that fumble with the Deb we were trying to delight. Thus, we had no good reason to believe holidays would be a panacea of excitement, just more huntin'/shootin'/fishin', along with going to the circus at Christmas, finding we were even more tongue-tied with girls, that Nanny wasn't indispensable, that your sister had adopted your dog.

And beyond? There was no Gap Year; instead, National Service loomed, then Oxford or Cambridge beckoned the brainier, a Guards regiment the rest; and, to the very few, the unmentionable thrall of a more lilac life in an almost club-like gay milieu. For four or five years Eton consumed our whole being. But some of us understood we had a lifetime ahead in which to roll, and rock, in the gutter.

SMALL WONDER

The Oldie

A review of *Ma'am Darling: 99 Glimpses of Princess Margaret* by Craig Brown

The subject of this book was a victim: of birth, circumstance, education (or sparseness thereof), romance, marriage, and her innate gaiety; but most all, of her stature.

Lifelong friends say that her diminutive size – far, far more than being number two, then three, then gradually further down-ranked – was what shaped her character.

Her grandmother Queen Mary teased her from earliest childhood. 'Ach, you tiny little thing, I can hardly see you', thus earning the tiny thing's undying enmity – and her stinging observation that 'Anyway, she was Morganatic, not really royal.' The opinion was often bruited throughout Mary's queenship. A close member of Princess Margaret's gang, Judy Montagu, heard a tiara'd old trout, gazing at a state portrait at Windsor, say, 'Poor May, with her Morganatic hands.'

Even the most glamorous years, her twenties, of Princess Margaret's film-star beauty, were marred by this lack of height; consistently remarked upon, initially with sympathy but later with cruel accuracy. It is no surprise that she was to develop a self-protective shell of aloofness. Contrary to royal blandness, she realised she had definite opinions and was going to voice them, and develop an aptitude for withering ripostes. Some unique, wayward gene seems to have been present in Princess Margaret's make-up.

Throughout history, royal ladies' sayings have been most memorable for their acid edge: the 'Let them eat cake' syndrome. Upstart Anne Boleyn was renowned for being 'rude and arrogant', Nell Gwynne impertinent, Wallis Simpson a trashy termagant, Queen Victoria (even shorter than Princess Margaret), instilled sheer dread in family and courtiers with her gimlet criticism.

It may be a cliché that smaller people are by nature aggressive, but it is only natural to find some way of holding one's own. In millionaires and movie stars, it may be mildly amusing; in paupers, it was deemed merely mockable 'Who does that little man think he is?' In princesses, it comes over as hoity-toity.

And humour wasn't prevalent in the family circle. Queen Mary had to prod her husband, when being told a joke, with her umbrella – 'Now, Georgie' – to extract the expected laugh. The Danish Court, Queen Alexandra's family, would sit around a table, each member counting. At ten, they'd all peal with laughter and start again from one (Alexandra herself thought the point of golf was to stop balls going in the hole, which she guarded fiercely, bashing each out of shape with her club). If humour was frowned upon, worse still was Showing Off. Both these sins Princess Margaret possessed in spades; both encouraged by her adored and adoring father.

'My Joy,' he called her (her sister, 'My Pride') and,

perhaps due to the King's man-crush on his equerry Peter Townsend, she was to experience the first bitter blow her birthright had decreed. An unsuitable suitor. The Group Captain seems to have behaved very shoddily; married, with children, and already attracted by another woman when courting his princess – who was, at the outset, seventeen and second in line. His charade continued until the inevitable 'mindful of my duty' renouncement, though she kept his photograph at her bedside for decades to come. Small wonder, then, her outlook became more guarded, her attitude more jaded.

American glossiness, on hold during the war, held as much attraction for Princess Margaret as it had for her abdicated uncle David in the 1930s. By the 1950s, slang and slingbacks, nylons and nightclubs, Broadway musicals and 'beat' (the Princess owned a record, 'Rock, Rock, Rock', released many years before Bill Haley clocked in) crossed the Atlantic, along with a new humour. The deadpan wit of Mort Sahl and Lenny Bruce, and the 'Insult Comics' Henny Youngman and Don Rickles was a far cry from Freddie Lonsdale's fluffy comedies or Lady Cunard's epigrammatic dinners. Even Coward, intimate with the family, himself the master-class in put-downs, seemed dated. Charming subtlety was being replaced by a more cutting edge.

Embracing all this novelty, and aided by the American ambassador's daughter, Sharman Douglas, Princess Margaret dazzled amid a set of white-tied toffs – known as the Wallace Collection, due to a leading possible suitor's name – though not one of them manned up enough to marry her, even if she'd have settled for such blinkered conventionality.

Inevitably, she met her match; someone she could give as bad as she got. For a while they played at being happy, but two eminently sensible children later, the match descended to *opéra bouffe*, now played to a jaw-dropped audience. One gets the impression that Roddy Llewellyn was the only man Princess Margaret truly, even selflessly, loved. There was no agenda in the romance for either, and her Marshallian-like acceptance of his marriage is genuinely moving, if yet another instance of her being a victim of circumstance, though not pomp.

But she was, after all, still the Queen's sister. Fawners and the flattered flocked, surprised at not being fawned and flattered back, but at being given a dose of often contrary opinions and criticisms; quite a change from the usual royal 'Have you come far?' rigmarole. Each tart comment was grist to diarists, as was her now less svelte shape and, of course, lack of height. But godchildren and old friends swear she kept her youthful, if acerbic, humour and style. Newer ones, the writer Selina Hastings among them, found her knowledge of history and literature inspiring.

Craig Brown has brilliantly drawn together the component parts of a complex woman in these quizzical, far-researched, often very funny, often sad 'glimpses'. His is an astute pen portrait of someone victim of not only herself, her role and her time, but of our – somewhat genteel – assumptions.

PRINCESSES

Harper's Bazaar

Thoughts on the film *A Royal Night Out*

Until her late teenage years, Princess Elizabeth, like her younger sister, the then Princess Margaret-Rose, had never once been abroad. The royal passion for visiting European relations at the drop of a tiara had faded out during their grandparents King George V and Queen Mary's reign, and they led a conventional family life at Royal Lodge, where, joined by their cousin Princess Alexandra, they played in the miniature house, Y Bythyn Bach, which still stands in the Windsor grounds, or when in Scotland, in a tin hut erected in the garden behind Birkhall, their home on the Balmoral estate. The years after the abdication and of World War II put the kibosh on any kind of educational jolly overseas. Sitting out the blitz in a blackout-windowed, bath-water-rationed Buckingham Palace prompted their father George VI to famously and endearingly remark, 'The poor darlings, they have never had any fun'.

That was to change with the coming of peace. As this film's story depicts, their first foray into London life was the night of VE celebrations, when their parents agreed to them mingling, incognito, with the celebrating crowds.

And soon, with their flawless complexions, tiny waists and glossy dark hair, the two sisters' arresting beauty captivated war-torn Britain as surely as any film-star. The Ritz, legendarily more fun during that time than ever before, and the nightclubs that had bravely stayed open willy-nilly, were magnets where Princess Elizabeth, more reserved and reticent – and some say already beguiled by Prince Philip of Greece – and Princess Margaret, already wearing 'quite a lot of makeup, and piercing cat-like blue eyes' as Cecil Beaton noticed – a laughing, dancing live-wire, could meet their contemporaries relatively informally.

And at parties as well; at these, in a London giddy with peace, uniformed officers mingled with white-tied scions, or at fancy-dress balls where they could both display their childhood skill at dressing-up (honed at those wartime pantomimes they produced to amuse their parents) and their shared brilliance at mimicry. At one such ball, given by the US Ambassadress for her daughter Sharman Douglas, the Queen went as a parlour-maid and Princess Margaret a Can-Can dancer.

Sharman became a lifelong friend of the both sisters, largely due to her novel, slangy, American humour and the wherewithal to import that rarest of luxuries, nylons, or the latest Broadway musicals; Margaret, a dab hand at the piano, would play the hits to her circle of friends – known as the Wallace Collection due to a favourite escort being Billy Wallace – and sing them at nightclubs such as Les Ambassadeurs, the Milroy, and The Four Hundred, where her table soon became known as The Royal Box.

Her days were often spent 'in a whirl, what with

rushing up to Lancashire, rushing down to Windsor, up
to Newcastle, back down to Windsor', as she wrote one
Easter to her close friend and erstwhile – their engagement was frequently rumoured – suitor Colin Tennant,
though soon, when he and 'the Wallace Collection'
put on a play entitled 'Lord and Lady Algy' for char-
ity, Princess Margaret was designated producer, aiming
darts of hilarious criticism at the society cast, Raine
Spencer (then Legge) among them, during rehearsals.
In a few months she was to continue her role of impresario on another production, The Frog, igniting her lifetime penchant for show-biz luminaries.

In 1947 when all four members of the royal family
sailed to South Africa, it was the first time the princesses
had ever left their homeland. On this visit, Elizabeth
made the memorable dedication to serving her country for her lifetime. And in the entourage was Group
Captain Peter Townsend. All-too-recent drama of the
former king and the divorced Wallis Simpson doomed
the romance between Townsend and Princess Margaret.
Some time would pass before her eventual marriage,
but in those intervening years her natural gaiety and
caustic humour enlivened British life as surely as her
sister's flawless ability as Queen.

PARK AVENUE PRINCESS

The Spectator

A review of *Helena Rubenstein: The Woman Who Invented Beauty* by Michele Fitoussi

In New York, in the 1960s, in a sleek, silvery elevator, I rose from the marble halls of Helena Rubinstein's gleaming emporium up towards the top floor office of a new friend who worked for that legendary beautician. Suddenly, unexpectedly, the lift stopped, the doors slid open and a tiny, squat figure with oily, inky hair scraped back and livid carmine cheeks above violently purple tweed capes, stabbed with a jagged, surreal brooch, stood peering up at what I hoped was my youthful, English-rose complexion. A short, intense scrutiny. Then, imperiously: 'Oy vey! But I sink ve can help. Tell Patrick he needs gif you our recipe. Now, out of my vay', she elbowed past me; we descended, not a word more, but not exactly in silence, for she was loudly sucking on a Lifesaver, and, by your leave, let go a none too discreet fart.

My unique encounter with the woman Cocteau called — and, given her machinations, not without a touch of irony — the 'Byzantine Empress of Beauty', encapsulated her self-made aura: her battle against blemishes, her extravagant style, canny acumen and her famously brusque manner.

The friend I'd been meeting was a tall, elegant and extremely witty Irishman named Patrick O'Higgins. To say he 'worked' for this *monstre maquillée* is not the half of it. He walked her, arranged her contracts, travelled the world with her, was the shoulder she cried on, made amends for her manners, held the heavily jewelled hand when husbands left and sons died. And he wrote an amusing, touching, critical but finally sympathetic book, simply titled *Madame*, about his many years with Helena Rubinstein.

Michèle Fitoussi's biography of the same subject puts much factual flesh on *Madame's* funny-bones. It is credibly researched, fairly accurate, without too many invented conversations and written in powder-pink, though somewhat cliché-ridden, prose. Exclamation marks dot paragraphs like beauty-spots, and there are more 'such as...' followed by lists of long-forgotten rivals than you can shake a lipstick at.

But Madame's story is one of resolute endurance. She was born Chaja Silberfeld, in Poland, on Christmas Day 1872, the eldest of seven sisters. Her mother boiled up a lanolin-based gloop that, once jarred, she slathered on the element-shrivelled skin of their Kazimierz neighbours. Chaja, now self-renamed Helena, saw a far wider clientele. Gathering up 12 jars of Mama's cream and 'armed with a parasol', she set forth, not to jaded Berlin or St Petersburg, but to newly-rich Australia, and an outback township above Melbourne at that. From here, she cabled Krakow with three little words: 'They need us.'

The creams arrived. Liberal additions of the abundant Aussie flora and fauna gave them fragrance and the lure of jeunesse. Toil in the back room of a wooden shack eventually led to a beauty parlour in Melbourne and the Governor's wife's patronage, some backing, the usual slew of hoary suitors, and her first husband, a US citizen called Edward Titus. Helena Rubinstein was ready to beautify Europe, America, the world.

With Titus in tow, Paris was her lodestone, heading straight for the Faubourg St-Honoré: but the bibliophile Titus, who in many ways is the interesting dark horse in the Rubinstein story — he soon befriended Proust, Colette, Man Ray, the Noailles and Louise de Vilmorin — preferred Montparnasse, opening a bookshop to rival Sylvia Beach's Shakespeare and Company, with his own press, The Black Manikin, publishing Gertrude Stein, Lawrence, Hemingway, Huxley and Samuel Beckett.

His circle gave Helena entrée to the major young artists, and, no slouch, she bought their work to hang hugger-mugger in her burgeoning palaces of powder and paint. She commissioned Louis Sue, Ruhlmann, Eileen Gray and Jean-Michel Frank among many others to design the various world-wide residences she would also cram with an unlikely mélange of African sculpture and Biedermeier bibelots, many bought from a young antique dealer named Christian Dior.

With France under her ruby-encrusted belt, Madame, leaving her many salons in the manicured hands of a trio of sisters imported from Poland, sailed for New York and 'the pitiful purple noses, grey lips .... their faces chalk white from terrible powder' of American womanhood. 'My dear, the United States could be my life's work.' And so it proved to be. In the twinkling of an eye, she'd opened an orientalist-themed headquarters, and 'wearing a tomato-coloured dress and eight strands of black pearls', she and Manka, another hastily summoned sister, displayed avant-garde treatment routines to cosmetically starved Manhattan ladies.

Salons proliferated States-wide, designed by architects Paul Frankl and Rudolph Schindler. Paintings by de Chirico, Tchelitchev and Marie Laurencin enhanced blue metallic walls. But Madame had a healthy disregard for her possessions. Many lurked in rarely opened cupboards, while, for the last of her famous alfresco parties at her property on the Cote d'Azur, she had her Chagalls, Monets, Renoirs and Modiglianis hung from the trees.

In the late 1920s, Rubinstein sold her company to Lehman Brothers, cannily keeping the stock. And despite two sons, she and Titus divorced. Some years later, past sixty and after a courtship of textbook corniness, she married Prince Artchil Gourielli – Tchkonia, an equally textbook dashing Russian émigré. Madame revelled in her title, bogus or not, mainly as it was one-in-the-eye for her only comparable rival, Elisabeth Arden. 'That Woman', as Helena referred to Arden, quickly responded by getting her own aristo, a Prince Michael Evlanoff. The two cosmetic queens' public mud-slinging and manager-swapping minefield has been hilariously detailed in Lindy Woodhead's earlier *War Paint*.

That book, and Suzanne Slesin's magnificent *Over the Top*, an all-encompassing photographic record of Rubinstein's extraordinary lifestyle, especially her huge, last apartment on Park Avenue (on being told 'no Jews', she bought the entire building), along with O'Higgins' bittersweet memoir, vividly demonstrate Madame's astonishing taste and restless determination. This book shows that Helena Rubinstein brought to the business something even she could not have realised would become so colossal: a lifelong, intense scrutiny.

IMMACULATE CONCEPTIONS

The Spectator

A review of *Making Magnificence*
by Christine Casey

Some thirty summers ago we were staying at a famously beautiful villa outside Turin. Our hostess was, indeed is, renowned for her superb taste and distilled perfection of every aspect of *douceur de vivre*. Each night we dined in a different sylvan setting, under inky trees, in flower-filled gardens, in C18th rococo salons amid porcelain bouquets of those selfsame flowers. Another, with candles lighting the Chinoiserie panelling, is forever incised in my mind, not merely for the decor as much as for the last course. In what appeared to be a vast rock-crystal bowl (in fact hand-frozen ice) was a fruit salad made solely of white fruit.... white strawberries and white raspberries from frames and canes, white peaches and white nectarines from glass-houses, white cherries, grapes and pears from orchards, white apricots from Armenia: pale as moonbeams, its contours gleaming, this creation was as refined as the frankly edible marvels of plasterwork illustrating this ravishing, erudite, book.

Refined, but clearly not in the genteel sense. To the ancients, white was the colour of heaven. So perhaps the fact that there is no true, pure, white — any more than there is true black — on Earth, made it nigh impossible, but highly desirable, to create it artificially. So doing had been the goal of the Western (the Chinese, conversely, associate white with death) civilisations for centuries. It was, still is, symbolic of immaculateness, that mystical yet ever-enduring ideal. The rarest things are white. Think of unicorns. Or ivory. Or white tigers and peacocks, white asparagus, and violets, stallions and ermine: the ceramics of Kaendler then and de Waal now, Samite on virgins and spotless linen on Beau Brummel, smooth snow and hard drugs.

Alchemists, having failed to turn base metals into gold, stumbled on a recipe for whiteness, which eventually brought about the manufacture of white porcelain. The gradual evolution from such decorative mediums as mud and clay led to a concoction of marble dust and gypsum. This near-white, plaster-like substance could be sculpted into statuary, as can be seen in the ostrich-feather head-dressed saints adorning Giacomo Serpotta's oratorios in Palermo, or in the following decades, applied to vast surfaces, such as the white triumphal staircase of Prince Eugene's winter palace in Vienna, and Maria Theresa's all-white state apartments at the Hradcany in Prague.

The protagonists of this elegant and fascinating book, however, worked with a far less sophisticated formula... a gloop made of sand, lime, glue, and indeed hair, which by some magic dried white. Armed with this strange recipe for *stucco*, as it became called, a group of young craftsmen from northern Italy pitched up in England and Ireland at the moment when rich milords, and architects — Adam, Gibbs, Carr and co., returned from their Grand Tours, were building Palladian-inspired mansions. And these *stuccadores* ornamented the newly erected domes, ceilings, friezes and over-doors with the long-coveted pallidness. Figures and fables, flowers and fruits, leaves and ribbons, all exquisitely moulded. And white. No colour to add eye-catching dimension, no gilding, was needed for these immaculate heavens hovering high above. In interior decoration at least, and at last, a pure whiteness had been realised.

Christine Casey knows her onions to a T. The flawlessly researched, erudite and entertainingly written text — much of it surprisingly gossipy in the sense of details about the *stuccadores* families — is accompanied by marvellous illustrations of both vanished and existing examples of their, and others, creations in this unsullied *métier*, all of them as visually delectable as that white fruit confection. My only quibble is with the book's title. It seems to me the whole subject is beyond 'magnificent', which implies some Versailles-like glitz. Maybe 'celestial' is the more appropriate word.

AMEN TO AN ERA

The Spectator

A review of *Patrick Lichfield:*
Perceptions by Martin Harrison

P atrick Lichfield — the outer man — wore his ego
proudly and loudly on his sleeve. And with his
aristocratic yet trendy good looks, his Harrovian
education, the brigade of Guards, his titled ancestry,
royal connections and friendships, his persistent anec-
dotal recall, his ruffles and velvet or leather and denim,
his stately pile, his dashing daredevilry, let alone his
reputed Lotharian appetites, one can hardly blame him.

Inwardly, perhaps, this braggadocio was a sal-
ad-days reaction, for Lichfield's youth was marred by
family problems. His parents divorced when he was
nine, his father's death clouded his coming-of-age; his
grandfather, wildly, decided to make the family home,
Shugborough in Staffordshire, over to the National
Trust. But luckily, as a child, Patrick was given a camera,
from which he was henceforth rarely parted. Not unlike
a Victorian predecessor, the Earl of Craven, he initially
photographed, subtly and playfully, the landscapes,
retainers and buildings of the Shugborough he so loved.
This perceptive, sympathetic approach, imbued with
gentle humour, suffused his future work, and this book
of his photographs is aptly titled *Perceptions*.

Perhaps because of this upbringing, Lichfield's work is, for the most part, essentially English in style. But he was uninfluenced by the surreal or rococo flourishes of the previous generation of British photographers — though there is a touch of Beaton in the portrait of Jane and Pandora Stevens — or the hard edge of contemporary newcomers, despite the fact that David Bailey, never a ligger for a lord, was a mate and admirer.

This could be due to the fact that Lichfield's sitters were, for the most part, already celebs. But however cosmopolitan those sitters, however warts-and-all the close-ups, Lichfield portrays them with his native, intrinsic tenderness. They appear unforced, unmanufactured, unlike the work of American photographers — Avedon, Penn, Rawlings — in the same period, though he could do that if he wanted; the fashion shoot on page 218 is certainly a nod to Avedon. His photographs also avoid the glossy intenseness of those of Roloff Beny, a Rome-based Canadian working in much the same field at the same time, or the disenchanted voyeurism of, say, Diane Arbus.

While not so supremely successful at taking groups as his contemporary, Snowdon — though Patrick's royal ones at least give us a schadenfreudian pleasure by necessarily including that rebel lord kitted out in those convention-shattering suede jerkins and turtle-necks — his informal pictures of the Queen must be the most delightful ever taken, especially that with her horse in the stable-yard at Balmoral. As a 'pap' he manages, unlike many, to get the atmosphere surrounding and emanating from the snapped: Mick and Bianca in their limo after their wedding — at which Patrick was best man — pulsate with hedonism, just as James Blandford's fluffed croquet-shot epitomises his lanky frustration.

It is these, particularly those in black-and-white, which capture that ever-hazier era. Dances, *granddames* and dames, dustmen and dukes, Speaker's Corner or silver-screen stars at the Savoy, hairdressers and hippies, vividly revive dimming memories. It is a kind of 'goodbye babies and amen' to the territory he covered, often astride his motorbike, to catch the misty expression of Susanna Yorke, the long, lithe, looks of Joanna Lumley or George Best, the Anouk Aimée-like beauty of Janet Lyle (compare the two), the Lartigue-inspired, statuesque stride of Loulou de la Falaise, baubled djellabas on tragic Talitha Getty, tiny mites at school on tropical Mustique gazing wistfully beneath wonderfully inappropriate posters for British Wool.

In the more formal and posed pictures, Lichfield managed to encourage the sitter's incipient humour, smiles, even grins, frequently a fraught problem with portraiture. Valentino, Roger Moore, Kenneth Clark, Boy George, a glistening James Coburn, a slyly card-sharping Duke of Windsor, even the curmudgeonly Dirk Bogarde, seem palpably to demonstrate what fun it was to be in front of Patrick's lens.

Whether this book elevates Lichfield to the level of 'great photographer' is for the reader to judge. There are certainly many more pictures by him that could have been included, had it been a bigger volume, such as those of his beautiful children and their mother. On a personal note, my company was asked, just after his death, to decorate, as a tribute to Patrick, a corner suite high in the recently rebuilt Mandarin Oriental Hotel in Hong Kong, a city he loved, and loved working in. We recreated his studio, copied furniture from it, his key lights instead of lamps, light-reflective umbrellas for shades.

With the help of his beloved Annunziata Asquith, we chose his most iconic photographs to put on the walls, a facsimile of his appointment book on the desk, and found his favourite books for the shelves. The wall-to-wall windows look down on that ever-expanding, breathtakingly night-lit harbour, which he enthusiastically photographed many times over the years. Due to that enthusiasm, these rooms are the most guest-requested in the hotel. Regardless of his utter Englishness, or his standing among his peers, Lichfield's admirers are legion, and his *Perceptions* will be studied and appreciated the world over.

A WAY WITH THE STARS

The Spectator

A review *of I Used to Be in Pictures:
An Untold Story of Hollywood* by Austin
and Howard Mutti-Mewse

Many people write, or at least used to write, fan letters to their film favourites. Usually all they received in acknowledgement was a 10 x 8 glossy with a mimeographed signature. A little persistence sometimes resulted in another, with a brief 'personal' message written by the ladies toiling in the fan-club HQs. Not so for the two authors of this riveting book.

The Mutti-Mewse twins, early on, became obsessed with all things Hollywood, firing off missives not just to the major stars but to every man they had seen or heard was connected to that once fabulous industry. They must have had a magic formula in their letters.

Replies flowed back hand over fist. Not just a signed portrait, elaborately photographed by Hurrell, Kesserle or Max Munn Autry in all the sender's splendour, but effusive messages of the 'come up and see me sometime' variety, and the authors — just them initially, but later with their wives and partners — scurried to these siren calls. And what makes their book so interesting is the fact that the twins were — are — clearly and touchingly fascinated by not so much the obvious huge movie icons, the Garbos and Grants and Dietrichs, but by the ones that had once been boffo until, to adapt Gloria Swanson in *Sunset Boulevard*, the pictures got bigger as they got smaller. And many of those silent stars who were unable — usually due to unintelligible foreign accents or a too-shrill tenor — to make the transition to talkies.

The Mutti-Mewses disinterred quite a few of these true old-timers, many, surprisingly, not holed up in some dingy aged actor's home, but living in Deco'd splendour in the Hollywood hills, or sprawling bungalows in the Palm Springs desert, and some even retaining the farms in New England, the year-round apartments at the Waldorf Towers, of their gilded heyday — evidently many of those 'three-pictures and phfft' players were nevertheless dab hands at real-estate.

Others certainly do live out their legend in retirement homes – among their rivals and visitors, pulling, like Anita Page — once MGM's greatest asset — a dazzlingly blonde wig and a canyon of carmine lipstick out of a Walmart carrier bag at the approach of either. And one can understand their vanity. While we have all heard of stars like Louise Brooks, or fiery Pola Negri, it's sad to realise the loveliness of one Ethlyne Clair or the perfect features of a mere B-movie player, Hillary Brooke, have been forgotten by all but themselves.

Many have wonderfully vivid pasts; Barbara Barondess, born in 1907 in Brooklyn, at six months was taken by her parents to their native Russia. With everything confiscated in the revolution, the family made it back to America, where Barbara was the only

American citizen ever to be detained on Ellis Island. Winning a beauty pageant and a screen test, she made minor films until retiring to become an interior decorator, with the Reagans, Greta Garbo and Marilyn Monroe among her clients. A certain Rebel Randall was as popular a second world war pin-up as Grable or Hayworth, while Paramount's Judith Allen would weep when recalling the demise of her Hollywood dream, having been 'run out of town' by Cecil B. DeMille, and beaten up by both her wrestler husband Gus 'the Goat' Sonnenberg and her boxer lover Jack Doyle.

Apart from the plethora of photographs of this uniquely American 'society', the authors transcribe, almost word for word, their meetings with their favourites. One Joy Hodges, a Broadway and film musical lead, for whom the song 'Have you met Miss Jones?' was written, takes them to the Thunderbird Country Club in Palm Springs and a blissfully *The Women*-like lunch, where a vastly bloated ('she eats too much Häagen-Dazs' says Joy) Ginger Rogers ('the gentlemen are asking about me, Joy dear') is, still, 'queen of the lot'.

Muriel Evans, the comedienne whose Norwegian accent entranced MGM bosses and made the rare crossover from silent to sound, recalls how Clark Gable would take out his false teeth, revealing a mouth of brown stumps. 'It gave him the bad breath that Vivien complained about whilst filming *Gone with the Wind* . . . a Hollywood big-man scared stiff of the dentist. Imagine!' And Mildred Shay, once Hollywood's 'pocket Venus' ('My tits were better than Hedy Lamarr's') in a cat-food-ridden, Wonderbra-littered, fading flat in Cundy Street, Pimlico, relives her affair with Howard

('ever a meanie with his money') Hughes, or describes
Errol Flynn's 'giant Johnny Dingle Dangle', and 'Tarzan'
Weismuller 'trying it on', the while devouring jumbo
packs of Rennies.

Of all these once-megastars, only Shay tells it like
Hollywood probably was: 'Everyone paints a pretty
picture, but it was raunchy and full of sex.' No matter. Austin and Howard convince us it was the field of
dreams we like to pretend.

DOUBLE VISION

The Spectator

A Review of *Beaton in Vogue*
by Josephine Ross

B y a fine coincidence, two legendary icons of British art were being feted in London on the same evening last month, and both are primarily famous, to the public at least, for their depiction of the Queen. At the National Portrait Gallery, the director Sandy Nairne hosted a dinner to celebrate the portrait oeuvre of Lucian Freud, while the Victoria and Albert Museum opened its major exhibition of Cecil Beaton's lifetime lensing of Elizabeth II.

In the 1950s these two artists were the epitome of London society. Beaton, by way of his groomed exquisite taste and laconic manner, was the epicene idol of sophisticated drawing rooms; the nascent Freud, 30-odd, untidy, brooding, supremely sexual, was a magnetic talisman for every smart hostess's house, and often her bed. It is quite clear, from reading biographies of the period, that when either appeared, conversation momentarily stopped, resuming on a heightened level.

The canny Beaton recognised Freud's allure, and soon asked him to dinner (at the V&A, the latter's name can be seen below Henri Cartier Bresson and Francis Bacon in Beaton's star-studded visitor's book at one such dinner in 1951) and also to pose (something Lucian was incapable of doing, it must be said), though it is perhaps telling that the resulting photographs do not appear in this paperback; most magazines, even three decades ago, when this book was first published in hardback, preferred less gritty subjects.

But though Freud had yet to achieve his supreme dazzling stature, Beaton, due to his photography, his drawings, his stage design, his film work and his writing, was already a legend. And *Beaton in Vogue*, containing as it does a huge cross-section of all these talents, shows exactly why. Of course there are all the famous faces and events of the 20th century. There are also delightful line drawings of people and places, each one demonstrating Beaton's acerbic eye and cartoon-like facility of draughtsmanship. Others, of the wartime Far East, for example, illustrate the quite considerable bravery needed to fly for hours in juddering prop planes to remote imperial outposts, with landmines and black widow spiders threatening his delicately desert-booted feet.

His camera work alternates, sustained right to the end of his career, between a kind of impish, almost amateur vision, and a more severe, studied romanticism.

His work is strangely un-fashion conscious; chic, certainly, but not defining modishness season by season. And even in close-up, his portraits lack the invasive cruelty most of the following wave of photographers went in for.

Not that Beaton couldn't be cruel; his writing — and one of the joys of the book is the many pages of columns and articles he wrote exclusively for *Vogue*

— certainly has a cutting edge. But that is a result of his gimlet awareness of the frippery and foibles around him rather than from any slashing of his nose to spite his face. His critical faculty was always to the forefront. Even those he revered came in for a drubbing — 'her mouth being knife-like, and lips perpetually moistened by her adder-like tongue' about his inamorata, Garbo, who playfully called him 'Beattie', is hardly the perceived view of the world's most famous 'recluse about town' as Gore Vidal succinctly put it.

Beaton also writes with easy vividness. In a thumbnail of Audrey Hepburn (whose legendarily elegant skin looks worryingly acne-fied on the cover shot) he describes her 'child-like head, as compact as a coconut with its cropped hair and wispy, monkey-fur fringe', which sounds like an early Freud drawing. And Mona Harrison Williams had a complexion of 'pink, and wet, marble'.

While this refreshing and vivacious publication is happily timed to coincide with Beaton's seemingly unending cache of court comings and goings, it is touching to see that it was originally published in his lifetime. Though by then he was manfully coping with the effects of a serious stroke, he was able to recall in what esteem he held, and was held by, his sitters, from Queen to commoner. And now a whole new generation can esteem him too.

DEADLIER THAN THE MAIL

The Spectator

A review of *Nigel Dempster and the Death of Discretion* by Tim Willis

This is an effervescent, elegantly written and faultlessly researched romp through the life and times of someone whose name in Britain was spoken with genuine fondness by an urbane few, with self-righteous anger by some and with disdain or fascination by almost everybody who can read — as, like it or not, very few people don't enjoy gossip.

Tim Willis has caught the atmosphere of the Dempster decades with uncanny precision. What now seems fascinating is that those not-far-off years, and whatever Nigel wrote all through them, suddenly seem so distant, archaic almost, and oddly innocent.

The title's 'Death of Discretion' exactly sums it up. If the war and its aftermath removed the awe with which aristocrats and heroes were regarded, and the stifling of upper-class scandal by patrician press barons (it seems incredible, now, that the public were ignorant of Mrs Simpson and the King until a few days before he abdicated), it was the arrival of the Sixties that meant everything was upfront and allowable. Circumspection went down the toilet with the pill, free love-making, stigma-less illegitimacy, Lady Chatterley and the end of censorship, leading to porn, drugs and the demise of our insularity.

Indiscretion, and the emerging spectre of instant celebrity, was the new tendency, though Dempster did not originate this. Rather, he realised that, to his readers, the formerly sacrosanct peccadilloes of elite and establishment figures were grist to a newspaper's mill. After a network call to friends in his circle, ever ready to dish the dirt, he would hint at such indiscretions in his column.

Many people judged Dempster to be a monster for these 'revelations', but looking back, one has to admit that there really were very few historically memorable scoops — Harold and Antonia, obviously, the Goldsmith war with *Private Eye*, Roddy and Princess Margaret (with not a little help from the lady herself) — and that none of the 'victims' could really claim to be scarred by them. Not unlike like his American contemporary Dominick Dunne, Nigel absorbed all he was told, indiscreet or otherwise, and stored it. And like Dunne, he only chastised in print those he thought deserved it: the self-important, the vain, the twisters of truth, the blatant liars.

But generally Nigel wasn't a thunderbolt-hurling Zeus of Fleet Street, passing judgment in the style of William Connor, who sensationally questioned Liberace's sexuality in the Daily Mirror (Liberace sued and won, inventing the phrase 'I cried all the way to the bank'). Many items in Dempster's columns presented both sides with fairness, and were written genuinely to help a small business, or to show concern for people — the doomed Myna Bird, for example, or the tragic Kanga Tryon — down on their luck.

He often padded with pap on 'the kinswoman of Lord Derby' level, the staple fare of his predecessors, whose hands were tied when it came to real scandals. It is gripping to muse on what Nigel would have done with the real humdingers of previous epochs: Unity Mitford, the aforementioned Wallis, the expulsion, in her gold-plated sharkskin-upholstered Daimler, of Lady Docker from Monaco, for tearing up its flag ('It's a dump . . . we're not going back to that dreary little country'); Christine Keeler; Margaret Duchess of Argyll and her photographs of headless naked men, and the long-running saga of Taylor going for a Burton.

During his decades in Fleet Street, Dempster came to learn almost everything about almost everybody — their beds of roses or their Achilles heels. More establishment figures than would care to be unmasked confided in him. But, apart from a few trusted cronies, he kept such information to himself. Unlike Truman Capote, he had the sense not to blow his cover, or his cred, or indeed his life, to smithereens with a Brit version of Capote's disastrous 'Answered Prayers'.

If the contents of his newspaper columns now seem ephemeral, it's his marvellous mocking contributions to Private Eye that are surely his monument. He was, along with the equally belligerent, brilliant Peter McKay, the trouble-shooter in that nest of schoolboy-humoured vipers, led by his 'hero', Richard Ingrams. Willis describes this involvement with insight and hilarity, and it was for Lord Gnome that Dempster flung darts with much deadlier accuracy than anything he put in the Daily Mail, where other writers' far unkinder, innuendo-ridden, wounding articles in the guise of investigative journalism were appearing with increasing frequency.

Willis's book treats the many facets of Nigel Dempster, his braggadocio and his bonking, his snobbism, his swagger, his guile and his generosity, from his colonial childhood to his almost state funeral in 2007 with frankness and in fascinating detail. Who'd have imagined one of Nigel's pre-prep school teachers was the father of the Countess of Wessex?

MAJESTY OF THE MALLS

The Spectator

A review of *Shop Girl* by Mary Portas

I n this autobiography, Mary Portas doesn't dip into
the fabled store of her talents by giving an account
of her countrywide progress as monarch and ora-
cle of retail, but conjures a nostalgic cornucopia of the
mid-20th-century brands and frankly cheesy TV per-
sonalities (she often dressed up as Jimmy Savile) that
dazzled her youthful Hertfordshire eyes. These were
rapturously set on future journeys, of which we get
only one — her great leap forward from North Watford
to Knightsbridge, where her undoubted brilliance as
a window-dresser eventually blossomed at Harvey
Nichols.

While credited with making that store a destination
experience — though possibly its acquisition by the
Hong Kong magnate Dixon Poon had a bit to do with
that — Portas certainly put the cat among the cushions,
but it always had a certain cachet. In the late 1950s,
Woollands, as it was then, was a Saturday morning pil-
grimage for the fashion elite, advertising moguls and
photographers, from the established John French and
Richard Dormer to the upstarts Bailey, Donovan and
Duffy, ooh-ing and ahh-ing at panoramas of hither-
to-unseen continental chic.

Mary's family, the Newtons — Brylcreemed dad, mum with a wisp of Goya's Coral lipstick, brothers, the altar boy Joe, police cadet-to-be Lawrence, Man-U obsessed Michael, future-nurse sister Tish — were the very model of that long-lost quality, civilised respectability. Mary, though fascinated by less routinely admired Hollywood movie stars like Hedy Lamarr and Carol Lombard and the arrival of glam-rock, was an exemplary student, and moved easily from Watford Comp to classier Rickmansworth Grammar. Intensely observant, every commercial product ratcheted in her mind, and part of the book's charm (and much of its index — even one bite of a Granny Smith gets a mention) is its litany of fondly remembered brand names.

And real-life names. Anyone Mary has ever heard of is there, from the milkman to the mega-men. A couple of years on she even got to meet one or two: 'It was only Malcolm bloody McLaren' who tapped enticingly on the plate-glass as Mary's team installed yet another eye-catcher. Outgoing, a natural performer and lured by fashion, Mary's lifeblood has always clearly been 'in retail' — an ambition that was encouraged in her cosy, tightly knit home.

Then it fell apart. Her mother died suddenly, too young. Mary comforted her grieving father, only to see him, a year or so later, fall for a stereotypically genteel bottle-blonde. He then married her and sold the family house, leaving his teenage family with nowhere and nothing. *Little Women*-like, Mary gathered the reins with capable hands while pursuing her artistic bent and becoming a locally envied, if outré, clothes-horse. 'Oxford bags, cream with large orange check, skimmed my skinny legs', and a Vidal Sassoon-inspired chick-yellow gamine crop set her on the golden road to SW1 and those department stores.

And pretty soon to a brief marriage with Graham Portas, whose 'lashes were as long as a cow's': it's a bit of a milk-sop ending. There's nothing further about Madly Modern Mary, the gender-bending, same-sex marrying, child-by-brother's-sperm-adopting, advice-dispensing, axe-wielding terror of the high street, quake-making queen of the malls.

The BBC selected *Shopgirl* recently as book of the week, read by Mary. She has a slightly irritating voice, but she overcame this hurdle by putting in plenty of expression, bathetic pauses and comic accents, the narrative relieved by added bursts of seminal pop-rock — not a bad idea, actually. But Auntie, by filleting any faintly contentious bits, managed to mould Portas into a Thoroughly Ordinary Person. We know, and she knows, that she is anything but.

HALLOWEEN HIRE

The Spectator

A review of *The Vulgar: Fashion Redefined* – an exhibition in The Barbican Art Gallery

To use a vulgar phrase, I can't get my head around this exhibition. It seems anything but 'vulgar'. Daintily laid out and dimly lit in the gloomier cloisters of Fortress Barbican is a series of dresses — the chaps hardly get a look-in, save for some of those white-knee-britched, jaboty, gold-laced-coat get-ups that people like Philip Green struggle into for their fancy-dress parties — some ancient, some modern, a lot very pretty, a few laughably ludicrous; anyone wanting a frightening clown costume for Halloween will find inspiration here. The clothes are, for the most part, exquisitely made. Many are elegant, and several supremely extravagant; however, the organisers of the exhibition seem to be trying to lump them all into the 'vulgar' basket. Which seems odd.

The earliest shown, those wide-panniered 'infanta' skirts (for keeping one's dwarf under?) with bosom-eliminating bodices, miraculous with their glittering appliquéd embroidery on wonderfully dull-coloured silks, are clearly works of art as much as fashion — as indeed are some of, say, Galliano's more extreme confections — but are they vulgar? There must have been a reason why they wanted this fantastic extreme silhouette. It could possibly have been religious. Did the Spanish court, where they originated, see their monarchs as being the embracers of their people, who could metaphorically shelter under those skirts, the Queen of Heaven protecting her flock?

There is almost always a reason why fashions evolve, just as in interior decoration; if one analyses the early shape of panelling — a rectangle with the corners scooped out — one realises that it's the shape of the animal hides our ancestors tacked up in their draughty stone huts. Columns are tree trunks, their capitals foliage, and so on.

There are a trio, if indeed you can see them in the murk, of peasant dresses from the Auvergne, refreshingly simple and perhaps the nearest thing to vulgar in its true sense of being 'echt', or grass-rooted. Advance a couple of centuries and Paco Rabanne's cream minidress – couture's antithesis of vulgar – stripped down much farther than Chanel ever dreamed of, is in the same galère, and a bit more shocking in its simplicity than any of the fantasy frou-frou that the next wave of designers indulged in. And I was pleased that my dear friend Rudi Gernreich, astonishingly one of only two Americans included — the other being Charles James, whose witty *Snow White*-print dress long predates the Warhol-stolen Campbell's Soup stuff — is represented by the very same tweed 'big pants', with nothing but narrow ribbon braces, that I'd had photographed on Rudi's muse and model, Peggy Claxton, for a spread in the US magazine I art-edited in the early 1960s. It was the first totally topless fashion photo ever printed.

There was a hue and cry at its publication. Many were shocked, but it wasn't actually considered vulgar. Maybe the vulgar can't be shocking, or the shocking vulgar. Vulgar is a weak current, boring, even; the shocking knocks your socks off. That is to a certain extent demonstrated by the most outré outfits the exhibition leads up to. We've known for years that they are rather marvellous, but they seem new now only because, as no customers ever seriously wore them, they were forgotten by all but fashion geeks — and were in any case created purely to get the paparazzi photo-op that would push the scent and sunglasses to the masses. Selling scraps of dreams: perhaps that is vulgar. And speaking of dreams, there's not a mention anywhere of Hollywood, where the clothes of Adrian, Omar Kiam and Travis Banton influenced not only European designers, but also women (and hence 'the vulgar') worldwide. If this exhibition had been done in the Diana Vreeland/Met mode there would have been some life to it, some eye-opening fizz, rather than textbook familiarity.

But is anything vulgar anymore? There's a quote by the curator Adam Phillips inscribed on one wall stating, 'Vulgar is the common tongue,' and here he has a point. Vulgarity has become the norm, even a sought-after quality. No one these days says, 'They're/that's so vulgar.' It would be far too un-PC. Women smoking in the street was considered vulgar in my youth, now it's about the only place they can. Wearing too few clothes in public isn't vulgar, nor is swearing, nor joking about death or illness. Being overweight is a 'problem', not vulgar, noisy children are just 'expressing themselves'.

Architects' ghastly new buildings go up without critical comment; appearing in rubber and bondage in public has taken the fun out of fetishism. One simply shrugs at the rock-bottom level of comedy on radio shows. Anna Wintour puts the Kardashians on the cover of *Vogue*; trillionaires' mega-yachts are envied, flashy lifestyles the fodder of tabloids; sportsmen spraying champagne is considered amusing. Restaurants with names like Sexy Fish get a nod-nod wink-wink.

It would be a relief if something actually was vulgar. Personally, I think *Bake Off* takes the vulgarity biscuit. I can't explain why. It just does. It's something to do with safeness, with appealing to the lowest common denominator. Maybe that's the message I missed in the show.

SHOCK AND AWE

The Spectator

A review of *Elsa Schiaparelli* by
Meryle Secrest and *Vivienne Westwood* by
Vivienne Westwood and Ian Kelly

A comet streaked into France in the 1930s, its fall-out sending the staid echelons of haute couture into a tailspin. A mere 30 years later a rogue missile blasted into London, blowing dainty English clothes sense to smithereens. Both these thunderbolts shot the stuffing out of cloying conventionality, one with an arrow-narrow silhouette, the other by blitzing the luxe out of luxury, the ex out of exclusivity.

It's worth studying the photographs of those two alien invaders, the subjects of these lengthy works. The young Elsa Schiaparelli, sleek-headed, confident, wearing strict black: and the young Vivienne Westwood, with tousled hair and a workaday high-street suit. Both have intense dark eyes with a far-reaching gaze above their determined mouths — ambitious egos, sisters perhaps, but over, not under, the skin.

'Comet' was the word Janet Flanner used in the 1930s to describe the arrival in France of the Italian aristocrat Schiaparelli. Secrest has enlarged on Flanner's diamond-etched essay, and trawled Elsa's autobiography *Shocking Life*, a matter-of-factly written work in which she rather weirdly refers to herself alternately in the first and third person.

Derbyshire-born Vivienne Isabel Swire's autobiography (her second, by the way, this one assisted by Ian Kelly), chronicles her slow rise from the village of Tintwhistle to punk *grande dame*, and takes the sledgehammer approach, resolutely in the first person. And boy has Vivienne got a lot to say — some of it defiantly honest, much of it on-trend guff. Rumours are swirling with accusations of plagiarism, about passages being lifted from another author; those parts may account for the book's pavement-slab weight.

There are comparisons to be made. They both benefited from muses – Salvador Dalí, among others, encouraging Schiaparelli to adorn her streamlined, Chanel-rivalling collections with unlikely motifs such as lobsters, frilled lamb cutlets and his signature chests of drawers, while Westwood's one-time husband Malcolm McLaren insisted on more subversive images with knobs on. Remember those cock-kissing cowboys, the exhortations to destroy, the safety-pin-lipped Queen, the S&M and the *nostalgie de la boob* T-shirts printed with disembodied breasts?

The difference is that Schiaparelli — let's call her Schiap, as she herself, her friends and contemporaries did — definitely influenced future fashion, particularly in Hollywood, where couturiers such as Travis Banton, Omar Khyam and Adrian were quick to pick up on her fluid, figure-skimming lines, backless dresses, reworking of furs and feathers, wide padded shoulders and oversized jewellery. For the best confirmation of her cinematic impact one only has to watch 'There's Beauty

Everywhere', the last segment of Vincente Minnelli's *Ziegfeld Follies*, a Dali-esque number in which Katharine Grayson sings in clouds of shocking pink soap bubbles, while behind her, on a painted desert, receding rows of chorus girls in Schiap-inspired satin sway surreally in a wind-machine created gale.

Westwood, however, was primarily, and self-confessedly, inspired by Hollywood, from James Dean's grunge to Errol Flynn's piratical swashbuckles. While Schiap looked determinedly forward, Westwood, with her bookworm bent, delved into and delivered witty, updated versions of *les Incroyables*, with crinolines and dirndls, and of course the corsets and bondage from which Schiap had so assiduously freed the female form.

There the comparisons end. Westwood, blessed with a stable childhood, clearly has a loving, caring nature and is able to draw the strands of her various relationships into an extended happy family, with hardly a bad word for anyone — with the exception of McLaren. Her well-publicised outrageous persona and opinions tend to belie her intellectuality, her knowledge of history, familiarity with the classics and her deep-seated social scepticism.

Schiap, on the other hand, had hardness in her ambition and a streak of cruelty, especially in her treatment of her polio-damaged daughter Gogo. She lived and worked and triumphed in that interwar period of gilded, globe-trotting art-and-café society, but one senses an underlying personal dissatisfaction. Her amorous relationships (and I was fascinated to discover we shared a lover) were haphazard, short and unsatisfying, though her friendships with women, particularly the dazzlingly beautiful and brilliant, but sadly unpublished diarist Bettina Bergery, lasted till her death.

Meryle Secrest, who has written trenchant, admirable biographies of Bernard Berenson, Leonard Bernstein and Modigliani, chronicles the intercontinental, party-giving, flippant (until Hitler came along) life of Schiap's Paris/New York/Los Angeles axis. The work and the dresses are described in intricate detail, though the prose sometimes lapses into *Bunty*-style exclamations: 'Even today — for a formal afternoon reception — the quintessence of chic!'; 'How could one resist?' and 'It couldn't be prettier!' Ian Kelly's interview technique is more wham, bam, thank you Dame. Though only three decades separate these two women, it's certain that they created fashions that startled their generations. But while Schiaparelli's most enduring legacy is 'shocking pink', Westwood's endearing punk is shocking to this day.

THE WORDLING'S PLEASURE

The Spectator

A review of *Lord of the Isle: The Extravagant Life and Times of Colin Tennant* by Nicholas Courtney

Two women are the only heroes of this book. One is Princess Margaret, whom the author points out was far more instrumental in the early years of Colin Tennant's ramshackle creation of Mustique than merely lending it her unparalleled presence. Quite apart from insisting, after Tennant had fallen out with a slew of architects, that Oliver Messel — now synonymous with the island's building style — become involved, she advised him on both possible investors and operators.

She also stuck by him through all his quixotic irascibility. For his part, he flattered, feted, and fawned on this major star of his Caribbean fantasy. The other hero — or heroine —is his wife. 'How wonderful Anne has been through all this,' people say. Nicholas Courtney's account of life with such an utterly selfish husband shows precisely how wonderful.

Tennant was quite clearly the most attractive, handsome, funny, odd, unpredictable and reckless creature of his time. And Lady Anne Coke, the beautiful and shy daughter of Lord Leicester, breaking the bounds of the sheltering stateliness of huge Holkham, fell once and for all for Colin's raffish magnetism, his elegance, his knowledge and his unpredictability. Through thick and thin, through bastardy and treachery, through celebrity and celebrations, through physical cruelty and family tragedy, even for richer, for poorer, Anne remained Colin's steadfast supporter and mainstay.

It can't have been at all easy, however, or glamorous. Colin, richly born into 'trade' money, but distantly related to what remained of old Whig aristocracy, and closely to that hyper-intelligent, if slightly self-conscious 'corrupt coterie' the Souls, had inherited many of the latter's traits; an amalgam of progressive thought, social-barrier breaking, classical knowledge and hifalutin intelligence, mingled with class security and provocative teasing.

This bloodline endowed him with searing intelligence, a steel-trap memory, profligacy, flamboyant taste and a fatal, for many, but specifically for Anne, enchantment.

Having lost his rag on the first night of their honeymoon, Tennant continued to lose it with anyone who disagreed with him, while charming those who didn't. An early foray into developing his family's holdings in the Antilles came to nothing, due to both these characteristics. However the tropics enthralled him, and having built a substantial mansion in Chelsea for himself and Anne, he hit on the desire for a tropical island fiefdom and quite soon found one for sale, albeit infested with mosquitoes. He blitzed it with DDT — after all, bugs can't be choosers — and began to build a harbour, import workers and stake out plots for future sale.

Within a decade, Mustique had become the most

covetable getaway for many rich and some famous — the most famous being in the hour-glass form of Princess Margaret. Having been given the most perfect plot on the island, the Princess, under cover of darkness, surreptitiously and sensibly extended the mark-out stakes — only to find, at dawn, the boundaries reinstated by Colin.

Her glamorous, if sometimes infamous, presence on Mustique lured the luminaries Colin needed; and the elaborate extravaganzas laid on for birthdays generated the notoriety he craved. But beneath these somewhat unreal revels lay the real troubles attendant on paradise. For all his show-off-manship, Tennant was a stranger to delegation; and one can't but feel sympathetically sad when his dreamland began to crumble, and was inevitably taken over by more stable though less sensation-seeking administrators.

Moving to the nearby island of St Lucia, Colin tried with dogged — or perhaps elephantine, as he imported one, called Bupa — determination to manufacture another magic kingdom, but his ever-fallible judgment, frequent furies and failing health began to its toll. Throughout these years, Anne, despite the devastating death of two of her sons, and the late discovery of an older son of Colin's by an early mistress, resolutely and bravely flew to his side, for the pleasures and unpleasantness Colin could still dish out in unequal measures.

More was to come. At the uncrating of Bupa, Colin noticed her immediate affectionate response to a young, illiterate St Lucian boy. Angrily dismissing two mahouts who had travelled with their huge charge from India, Colin installed Kent Adonai as the elephant's chaperone, and gradually as his own. Soon Kent was assisting at every level with the administration of various St Lucian ventures, joining Colin on visits to London and Glen, the Tennant family home in Scotland, to Italy, and to India.

The family sighed with relief; Kent could calm Colin's infuriated outbursts and reign in his extravagance. By now gradually toothless, and seemingly more clawless, he appeared resigned to an old age passed between the twin peaks of the Pitons, more genial to associates, more fond of his family, his collected treasures around him. The shock that at his death he left nothing to any member of that family, including Anne, was profound; more unfathomably, he had willed everything to Kent Adonai.

Perhaps we should not be surprised. As the author makes clear, his subject all too frequently pulled the rug from under his own feet, as well as those of anyone who became close to him. But what a vivid tapestry Colin Tennant wove with his life, even if the threads were tarnished with self-absorption. And that fatal enchantment.

FLAPPERY WILL GET YOU NOWHERE

The Spectator

A review of *Flappers: Six Women of a Dangerous Generation* by Judith Mackerell

I'm never quite sure what the term 'flappers' means. How did these creatures flap, and why? Where did they flap? Did they flap all day, or only at night? Were they in a flap, or being flapped, sad-flaps or flap-happy? Did they open flaps, or close them? Did they flap Jacks, or flip Jills, or both?

Reference books don't help much. The *OED* says the word means a fly-killer, and you really don't want to know the *Dictionary of Slang*'s definitions. So what was, in the accepted vo-deyo-do-ing, headache-band-browed, fancy-dress costume and Baz Luhrmanesque image, a 'flapper'?

One might assume that in this substantial, erudite and detailed, but oddly humour-free book, Judith Mackrell would set out to enlighten us. But instead she focuses on six women, each renowned in their own way, 'of a dangerous generation', as her subtitle has it. The 1920s were essentially their early adult years, but surely that decade was less dangerous than the one before it, or those to come?

Like the relieving interval in some interminable opera, the author breaks her subjects' stories into two five-year chunks apiece, in which each one's life (practically day by day), parents, affairs, marriages, correspondence and thoughts are delved into in lengthiest detail, fleshed out by what we already know of them through several biographies, not to mention memoirs and autobiographies.

Admittedly these women were headstrong, original and groundbreaking — I fear the word 'empowered' lurks somewhere in Mackrell's prose — but she somewhat arbitrarily pins the badge of flapper onto some really rather serious lapels. I mean, Diana Cooper, most unrufflable of characters, a *flapper*? Or the deeply, darkly, socially-conscious Nancy Cunard?

Nor, surely, did the term apply to Zelda, one half of the most irritating — *pace* their literary output — couples of the time. What with the Fitzgeralds' falling out with each other and falling into bed with everyone else, their droning rows, their drinking bouts, their flocking to fashionable faces and places, there was little time for Zelda to flap, though plenty for self-dramatisation.

The book's cover-girl, Josephine Baker, sleek in a slippery silken negligée at the Folies Bergère, was more famously near-naked in that bouncy banana kilt (suggested by Jean Cocteau — 'on you', he told her with typical irony, 'it will look very dressy'). She moved with such lithe, wild-creature-like grace that both philosophers and playwrights agreed that she ceased to be merely erotic but 'clothed in unselfconscious dignity'. When she did dance in all those feathers, it was onstage at the Casino, though as the *New Yorker*'s Paris correspondent Janet Flanner observed, 'on that lovely animal visage now lies a sad look, not of captivity, but of dawning intelligence'. Offstage, she was far too busy to flap, learning the lingo of her *pays d'adoption* ('at first she couldn't even speak American', said her nightclub-owning rival, Bricktop) and later adopting a Baker's dozen of orphans from other, far-flung, *pays*.

Less dignified was Tamara de Lempicka, a somewhat lumpen Russian refugee with a small talent for painting large, glossy, cubist portraits. Tamara dutifully studied with minor modern masters until a failing marriage and an obsession with glamour led her into the first of many lesbian affairs in the Sapphic circle round Natalie Barney; eventually, scoring *nil points* in Gertrude Stein's flapper-free salon, she had a go at the tiny, and probably gay, Risorgimento poet and tyrant, Gabriele D'Annuncio.

Of the six, one could make the most convincing case for Tallulah Bankhead being a sort of flapper, though that most rewardingly sophisticated of stars would never have been so banal as to fling strings of pearls over her shoulders while black-bottoming in satin kitten heels, like Clara Bow, Hollywood's *echt* flapper — who does rate a passing mention. But Joan Crawford, who, while making her youthful fame and fortune dancing a frantic Charleston on flickering celluloid, particularly in *Our Dancing Daughters*, and famously knickerless, rates none.

Incidentally, films of people doing the Charleston are usually sped up. Originally it was danced quite slowly, and often cheek-to-cheek, so perhaps our dancing aunties were not such lively hoofers as we fondly picture them.

Anyway, there's hardly a hint of liveliness in these

deathless pages, and despite its title, as a guide to the 'It-girls' of so many decades ago, the book falls all a bit — well — flap.

TALKING PICTURES

The Spectator

A review of *Cecil Beaton: Portraits and Profiles* edited by Hugo Vickers

B eaton was the great inventor. Apart from inventing not only himself but his look, his voice, his persona and a glamorous family, he invented the Rococo in photography – the Edwardian period for the stage and films, the most outré of costumes, the elaborate for his rooms, a cartoon-like simplicity for his drawings, and the dream of being a playwright and painter. What he didn't need to invent was being a writer, at which, as his many books, and particularly this one prove, he was a natural.

His lifelong observance of the world around him gave him the power to describe on paper, always acutely and often superbly, landscapes, cities, colours, nature. And, of course, people. He was a snob, but not snobbish. Alice B. Toklas ('fatter and more hirsute') noted that while the young Princess Marina, Duchess of Kent, was wildly enamoured of him, Beaton preferred the distinctly *distrait* allure not only of Greta Garbo — 'incapable of love' and pictured sitting glumly on a sofa in wellingtons (surely a template for that recent *Vogue* cover of Posh Spice?) — but also, it has recently been suggested, a tougher tumble with 'pallid as a mushroom' Marlon Brando.

He could hone in on the fineness or flaws of friends or foes with a pen not dipped in scented flattery or wounding venom (except about Coco Chanel), but with enough vinegar to give piquancy to his words. He astutely sums up the-then Mrs Simpson's 'rugged mouth', and paints an indelible word-picture of the young Katharine Hepburn, with 'her beetroot coloured hair and rocking-horse nostrils'; though later he might have been more derisive. I once saw him stick his tongue out at her receding, snarling figure after a particularly stormy Coco costume discussion. Mick Jagger's skin is 'chicken breast white', Mae West he found 'a nice little ape', and in the teenage Princess Margaret he observed 'no interim between a shut, serious mouth and a flashing grin', an early, and neat, summing up of her 'girl-with-a-curl' personality.

The Beaton industry has been working overtime this year, what with a brilliantly original exhibition of his life in his two Wiltshire homes, Ashcombe and Reddish, at the Salisbury Museum, and another of more familiar photographs wittily mounted by Jasper Conran at Wilton House. But Hugo Vickers has crowned it with this beautifully produced — *pace* some rather cod attempts at imitating Beaton's own carefully achieved, wonky handwriting for the headings — volume of his most iconic sitters. It contains no images of his travel and war work, to achieve which he showed astonishing bravery — night-flying, strapped into creaky bombers to battle situations in, say, Libya, is hardly the activity one associates with the creator of these polished portraits. There aren't many we haven't seen before though a candid shot of Stephen Tennant in (where else?) bed seems unfamiliar if not exactly visually fresh. And while they encompass his, and indeed — except for the very young — our age, Beaton's words frequently speak as loudly as his actions.

UN-BEATON

The Spectator

A review of *Beaton at Brook Street*, an exhibition at Sibyl Colefax & John Fowler

The odds were a hundred to one against him. Brought up in bourgeois Bayswater by genteel parents, Cecil Beaton was effete, pink-and-white pretty, theatrical and mother-adored, with a stodgy brother (but a couple of compliant sisters) —a cliché of post-Edwardian sniffiness, a leer through raised lorgnettes.

A humdrum early education followed by Harrow might have formed him into a pliant carbon of his timber-merchant father, but Cecil escaped this. His personality, energy and burgeoning bravery led him far and wide, and often delightfully astray. It took just a few years for him to trample those early 20th-century taboos under his winged heel, and forge his curiosity-fuelled career.

Armed with a brownie and a box of cellophane, spun-glass wigs, beauty spots and chutzpah, he ditched the rigid formal poses of the period and carved his niche in portraiture and fashion. Swayed by the glamorous sheen of Baron de Meyer's work, Cecil's was a fusion of Elsie Mendl's Louis-the-Rococo, Syrie Maugham's bleached modernity and the vibrant notes of the jazz age. There were others in this fraternity, Peter Rose Pulham and Angus McBean among them, but it was Cecil who left his hallmark on the period. Stage and film design followed, and then, thanks to an acute ear, tongue and eye for observing human strength or frailty, his writing. What has been largely overlooked, though, is his genius for interior decoration, which an exhibition of his two Wiltshire country houses, Ashcombe and then Reddish, at the Salisbury Museum earlier in the year, and now at Sibyl Colefax & John Fowler, ably redresses.

The first room of Cecil's I saw was in the mid-1950s. He was, by then, at the crest of fame and taste, both of which are given rein in these interiors. After war-torn years of dingy walls and rep curtains, the opulence of his Ritz Hotel-Edwardiana drawing-room in Pelham Place was breathtaking, and, as I later wrote, 'walled in crimson velvet, gilt-mirrored and candle-sconced, containing an armada of *capitonné* crimson damask-covered, tasseled furniture skittering across Savonnerie carpets and gleaming parquet, ceiling-brushing palm trees in Chinese vases, bronzes and bibelots on myriad marble surfaces, and in it, Cecil, a lilac-suited figure in a rose-red bower...' 'Well, I think it's got something,' he said, in response to my stunned appreciation. I'll say.

But I was lucky to see that first incarnation, for he was planning a different something; while away in New York designing *My Fair Lady*, the house was to be transformed. My next visit revealed black-velvet walls with silver-gilt leather borders, Alberto Giacometti bronze lamps, and Jean-Michel Frank's plaster lanterns hanging above angular banquettes and chairs covered in clashing pink and orange, sky-blue and turquoise tweeds and silks. Years later, after Cecil's death, I was able to rent the house with this daring décor still intact. It hadn't dated an iota. If anything, current taste had caught up with it.

On his regular visits to New York during the time I worked on *Vogue*, Cecil would be installed in rooms he had designed at the St Regis hotel. A far cry from the pastel panelling of its neighbours, Cecil's suite was daringly modern, with splashy black and white upholstery, vibrant slashes of primary colours, and, as far as I remember, huge photographs — not necessarily his — on white walls. Those primary colours he reserved for indoors. Visiting my ranch in Arizona, his nose twitched on seeing my proudly cultivated tubs of geraniums; then, *sopra voce*, 'Do they HAVE to be red?'

At Reddish, his last home, elements of all these earlier décors fused. Cecil's taste was now surer, perhaps even more serious. There was a final fanfare of Edwardian pomp for the drawing room, but quieter circumstance prevailed in the other rooms. This last house was to be no fantasy, but a suitably workable one, where he and his guests would be surrounded by the best furniture and art of periods that Cecil's exacting eye had chosen. Any dross was eliminated; only old and new rarities made the cut. I was able to acquire one or two things at the sale of his possessions, memento mori of the man and the magic, but looking now through the Christie's catalogue one finds, buried among the best of French and English furniture and paintings, more recent names — Picasso, of course, and

Tchelitchew, and then Hockney and Warhol. And 'Lot 473 ...Vase and two figures by Giacometti'.

Its counterpart was sold in New York this week for $101 million. The odds certainly weren't against Cecil.

HIGH SOCIETY

The Spectator

A review of *The Astaires: Fred
and Adele* by Kathleen Riley

O ne evening in 1923, Edward, Prince of Wales,
pretty as paint in his white tie and a cutaway-coat,
went to the theatre to see a new Gershwin musical. It was called *Stop Flirting*. Always one to ignore
instructions, the Prince returned to enjoy this froth no
less than nine times more. Obsessed by anything and
eventually, disastrously, anyone American, the heir to
the throne was fanatical about the new-fangled craze
then being displayed at the Shaftesbury Theatre by a
dazzling young brother-and-sister act hot-foot from
Broadway: ballroom dancing.

Practising the Charleston and the Black Bottom
rather than studying charters and red boxes occupied
the heir to the throne's days, to the intense irritation
of his father. Edward 'continues to dance every night.
People will think he's mad ... or a bounder', George V
fumed to the Queen, adding laconically, 'Such a pity.'
In the meantime, with friends like the Mountbattens or
Thelma Vanderbilt, his son would foxtrot and quickstep
in one or other of the newly fashionable nightclubs
— the Embassy, Kit-Kat, Riviera or Ciro's — until the
waiters piled up the chairs.

Now the future king was to succumb to the tidal wave of 'Astairia'. After several visits to *Stop Flirting* he befriended these comets of musical comedy, the dazzling Adele and Fred Astaire, toast of America and Europe. The attraction was mutual — Adele was rather taken by Edward's favourite brother, George, Duke of Kent — and after their performance the Astaires would often join the royal table at a nightspot; as dawn flushed over the West End, the Prince would ask them back to St James's Palace to punish the parquet with the latest steps.

Besides dancing, Fred and the Prince had much in common. Their shared passions included somewhat outré clothes; both men were small but well-proportioned, and Fred was soon aping the royal style, having his suits made by Edward's tailors, Anderson and Sheppard, using his shirt and shoe-makers, and even taking hero-worship so far as trying to walk and talk like the Prince.

But there was more to their mutual attraction than tailoring and tap. They each had overpowering mothers — Mama Astaire, Ann Austerlitz, sounds every bit as steely as May Saxe-Coburg-Gotha — who treated their sons as little boys, believing they could control their careers. Both men were strongly drawn to the company of older women and both mothers abhorred this predilection for married ladies. Queen Mary never met any of Edward's inamoratas, from Freda Dudley Ward onwards, and Mrs Austerlitz was distinctly distant to the divorced Phyllis Potter whom eventually Fred did marry, though both his mother and his sister openly suspected that Fred was homosexual.

Adele, with her enchanting looks, sublime figure and lightening wit, was by far the most popular — worshipped would be more accurate — of the two. She had the supercharged, naughty sexuality Fred lacked; she 'assisted Cecil Beaton to dispose of his virginity', Howard Dietz, co-author of the Astaires' later hit *The Band Wagon* wrote, noting that she also enjoyed the good spanking he himself would administer when she was late for rehearsal. Added to all this was her notoriously filthy language: Fred and his friends called her Lady Foulmouth. (Having met her, by now Mrs Kingman Douglas, in Jamaica many years later, I can attest to the veracity of these assertions)

In this well-researched book, Katherine Riley thoughtfully evaluates how essential she was to the Astaires' ten-year dancing partnership, and how distressed Fred felt by Adele's decision to abandon their act and blatantly ask the ninth Duke of Devonshire's attractive, albeit alcoholic, son Lord Charles Cavendish, who was working at J.P. Morgan in New York, to marry her. He accepted, calling the next morning to tell Adele: 'If you don't marry me, I'll sue you for breach of promise.'

Notwithstanding intense disapproval of the match from the Cavendish family, and the inconvenience of the wedding being postponed for a fortnight while her daughter's fiancé was hospitalised as a result of excessive drinking, Ann Austerlitz obtained a licence for a ceremony in the private chapel at Chatsworth in which, astonishingly, no marriage had heretofore taken place. Moucher Duchess of Devonshire recorded Adele's impact on the family: 'All gathered, like stone pillars in the library, the heavy doors opened and there stood this tiny girl, beautifully dressed. We waited for her to approach us, but instead of walking she suddenly began turning cartwheels.'

Everyone loved it.

The old Duke, thus beguiled by Adele, was appalled to find she was a Roman Catholic, so on the morning of 9 May 1932, as she prepared for her wedding, in 'beige satin by Mainbocher, with touches of orange at the waist and a set of blue fox furs', Adele was received into the Church of England. That afternoon Lord and Lady Charles Cavendish sailed for Ireland, to the magical castle at Lismore, once Sir Walter Raleigh's. Adele loved Lismore and when, in 1944, Charlie died there with mother-in-law Ann at his bedside, Adele noted wryly the irony of so historic a house being in the custody of a 'hoofer from Nebraska'.

The hoofer's brother, meanwhile, had abandoned the stage for the movies. That even more famous partnership nearly wasn't. 'What's all this talk about me being teamed with Ginger Rogers?' he railed at his agent. 'I will NOT have it. I did NOT go into pictures to be TEAMED with her or anyone else.' The author makes the point that Fred without Adele felt uneasy at being hitched to a brighter star.

Meanwhile, his own was on the rise. Marriage had produced a daughter, Ava, and his byword chic had eclipsed even his sartorial mentor, the by-now Duke of Windsor. Riley documents his touching sadness at the death of such friends as George Gershwin. She also comes up with some wonderfully arcane showbiz trivia. Who could ever imagine that 18-year-old Adele's first 'crush' was a Spanish dancer named Eduardo Cansino, whose daughter would one day be Fred's glorious co-star, Rita Hayworth?

But of the two siblings, Adele is the most enchanting. 'Jack just adored her,' President Kennedy's sister-in-law Lee Radziwill recalls. 'And they didn't even sleep together.'

FISH AND CHAPS

The Spectator

A review of *The Day of the Peacock, Style for Men 1963-1973* by Geoffrey Aquilina Ross

This is the ultimate 'niche' book. It focuses on that singular decade between the years of rockers and punks when toffs, freed from school or army uniforms, and toughs, discarding skinhead aggression, found a sartorial meeting point.

This new style, the cool child of late Fifties mods, had been given a huge public oomph by the Beatles and 'their silly little suits' as David Bailey (who has stated that he, along with myself, was the unwitting originator of the look) succinctly puts it. It was sharper, leaner and hinted at androgyny. Its creators were no longer found in caverns down Carnaby Street, nor high in the King's Road, but centered around that time-honoured dandy's inferno, Savile Row.

Certainly West End tailors had been turning out the archetypal three-piece for decades, but the author makes the somewhat dodgy statement that the Duke of Windsor's clothes were 'classical'. Classical? Those huge clown-check plus-twos and fairy Fair-Isle pullovers? And he maintains that teddy-boy gear was Edwardian inspired — though I would say it was more Mississippi river-boat gambler/western sheriff. The real retro Edwardians were that cast of hour-glassed figurines, Peter Coats, Bill Akroyd, Hardy, Cecil, Bunny et al, whose suits were wildly exaggerated versions of what clubland codgers had worn for a century and still are wearing, though somewhat whiffily, dry cleaning having always been absolute athenaeum to St James's habitués.

Around this time there were two (unmentioned) pretenders to the Peacock Throne: the 'dandy' Kim Waterfield wore gleaming white suits, while Kenneth Tynan (whose middle name was, appropriately, Peacock) wore flamboyant turquoise, liberally doused with Guerlain's *L'heure bleu*.

But Geoffrey Aquilina Ross misses an important point: the sudden change in female fashion during the period. It was only now that women were being allowed into hotels and restaurants wearing trousers. As girls began to dress like boys, the boys started flirting with paler colours and softer materials. *Vogue's* cookery writer, Lady Arabella Boxer, on seeing Christopher Gibbs in a subtly hued *tailleur* exclaimed, 'Goodness Chrissy, what a pretty trouser suit.'

Given that this style was different, focused, individual and very new, it seems odd that the cover shot – fuzzy at that – shows Michael Fish, the movement's ringleader, looking more like a cross between Oscar Wilde and Radclyffe Hall. But the chaps get better inside.

There's a touching spread of the members of a new model agency, 'English Boy'; almost all of them whey-faced, stick-thin, coked-out beauties, as indeed many of them are still today. Their appearance quickly relegated chiselled regular-guys like Roy Nightingale and John Blamey to the Daily Express's dustbin. There is Patrick Lichfield, as ruffled, jewelled and cuffed as Liberace before him or Adam Ant after. There is the creator of those very ruffles, Annacat's Janet Lyle, at the height of her sensational beauty, and a whole slew of angular aristocratic Ormsby Gores, their profiles and limbs as defined as stained-glass saints. There is Barry Sainsbury, whom Beaton thought the best-looking man he'd ever seen, and sometime financial half of the Fish shop; and of course Mick in the white gauze dress Fish made for that Hyde Park gig. There's also the taut athleticism of Rupert Lycett Green, whose premises, Blades, at the gate of Albany's rope-walk, verged on a literary salon with a tattered Thesaurus for a door-stop.

As I was living in cowboy kit in Arizona at the time, Blades would be my immediate off-the-plane date. Rupert made me the first ever black velvet dinner-suit for a ball in Venice. A dazzlingly handsome young man complimented it. 'Ravissante! May I copy'? He was Valentino. Later I grazed my knee and tore the velvet. Rupert mended it with a pre-punk patch of blue denim.

The author has assembled many fascinating and nostalgic facts to accompany the photographs, all of which combine to show how uniquely English his subject is. Pierre Cardin's collarless chinoiserie, and the space-age plastics of Courrèges had little impact on this island's phenomenon. We see that the peacock decade had softness in its sharp edge; conventions were stripped out and elegance created via daring cut and detail.

Sadly, however new, however fearless, however groundbreaking this tailoring was, by the end of the decade it was a dead duck. Jeans had taken over, suits reverted to dull necessity. Until, that is, Armani, Gucci and Tom Ford (not forgetting my personal Valhalla, Topman) came along to make clothes that gave the peacock in English lads a new proud strut into the 21st century.

DRESSING FOR DINNER

Tatler

We had flown from Northolt, at that time London Airport, and called an Aerodrome. The B.E.A 'plane, with thinly upholstered, exposed metal seats, had been, I suppose, hastily converted from troop-carrier to this civvy luxury. We shook and rattled across to Le Bourget, likewise Paris' only passenger terminal. It was 1947, and my first experience of 'abroad'. My mother, who had a bit of a thing about France having lived there in early childhood, was buffing up her French, rusty after war years, with two French lesbians – yes, even aged eight I could tell – in the row behind.

I think she chose to go to see the recently revived collections as an excuse to be back. She wasn't, at heart, a couture creature. And clothing coupons, used for my brothers' school uniforms, had put paid to such frivolity as fashion. She had, like most wartime women, a good coat – hers was red, and A-line – for going up to town, and something long and dark for evening, though my father resolutely stuck to black tie while bombs dropped in our woods. But four little words had blown across the Channel, and she, like a thousand others, had breathed the air bearing them...Christian Dior, and New Look.

How she got this whole scam past my father in the

teeth of true austerity beats me. We stayed at the Hotel Scribe, toweringly grand and creamy after the grime of London. The halls glittered with vitrines, jewels, and gloves, and scent and stockings, and in one bonbon-niere I distinctly recall boxes of pale, green, almond-paste chestnuts, prickles-and-all perfectly crafted and coloured, some half-open to reveal the chocolate conker within. But no time for dallying. Off to the Avenue Montaigne and M. Dior's salon.

Of course, after some seven decades, my memories are mingled with the many photographs of that fabled salon. But I can see, feel, scent, now, the warm grey, the bold white, the rows of gilt chairs facing the defilé, on each a list of the names of the dresses that would soon appear between the palm-edged velvet portières, 'Longchamps', say, or 'Rêve de Violettes' and 'Patachou'. And while, to modern eyes, the mannequins wearing them could look strangely elderly, they were appro-priate for the clientele: their perfect figures and delib-erate walk, faultlessly displaying the cut, the flow; the chien seemed goddess-like, a siren's call far from frosty modes in war-torn Bruton Street windows.

Dior's creations themselves were of less interest to me than these sublimely elegant creatures, or the murmured approval among the extravagance-starved clientele as a new creation appeared. My mother stud-ied each of them, but maybe due to her preference for something simpler, their sheer volume and perhaps their already-famed new length harked back to the fashions of her youth. Instead, she bought a tailored black dress, daringly and asymmetrically fastened down the back with oversized buttons, cinched by a wide belt proclaiming '1948' in large golden nail-heads...and from Jacques Fath.

Happily, I was able to make up for her turncoat decision. Little more than a decade later, after a lunch in Chantilly, I drove into Paris with Lilia Ralli, Dior's *directrice*. Figi, as everyone called her, suggested that if I was in Paris that week, to come and see the *defile*, as 'M. Dior has taken on a brilliant young assistant, Yves St Laurent'. I was leaving the next day, but Figi's words had stuck, and I was aware, within months, of Yves' rocket-ride to couture heights. By now I was working at American Vogue, and yakked constantly to Mrs Vreeland, to who Balenciaga and Givenchy were the zenith, about him. Pretty soon she was won over and YSL was on Vogue's every page.

Diana must have told Yves of my enthusiasm. On his initial visit to New York, he asked me to dinner 'in gratitude'. We went to Le Pavilion, where I had been once before; with Mainbocher, the great couturier to a previous generation. Yves and I dined alone, the restaurant lit entirely by candles, as it was the night of the great electrical 'brown-out', with not a single light in all Manhattan.

Floppy-haired, tongue-tied, gentle Yves was later to burn his candle at many ends while burnishing his genius; Dior's was already legendary. But this glimpse, however infinitesimal, of their shared charisma is still vivid, from one blustery morning at Northolt aerodrome to a candlelit evening on 57th and Park.

GARDENS AND GODS

Milieu Magazine

There has, surely, been a building of some description on this vineyard-ringed estate for many centuries. Against a steep flank of the Alpes Maritime, its wooded silhouette rises, acorn-oval and somewhat higher than the surrounding foothills, to a summit as neatly flattened as a child's sandcastle. Nature and man must have colluded to create so civilised a setting, with a wide, clear outlook across upland meadows and pine-crested knolls. In the distance, ravines and rivers run down to the coast. All along that shore ran the Via Aurelia, the golden road, constructed to march Caesar's legions from Rome to Arles, the far-flung Second Capital of the Empire, while on some high hilltops we can still see their temples.

Over time immemorial, this hill must have begged to be adorned; an incised pagan stone, and then a row of classically fluted columns: perhaps, later, a turret or cloister...the spread of Christendom may have given property its centuries-old name, Le Mas Notre Dame... and finally, pale ochre-washed and grey-shuttered house surrounded by a garden impressive both in scale and vision and simplicity.

I can write those words only because so ambitious an undertaking would have been way beyond my horticultural prowess. The owners, over the several years since they acquired the property, had learned exactly what thrives where and blooms when, and having quit the financial roots they had ruled, decided to create, over time, this very original garden, which still, each season becomes ever more refined due their exacting eyes.

My first, and almost only physical contribution, was to insist that a vast, shallow and leaky pond in front of the house should be removed...from the start I had an idea of a row of stone urns amid box, defining what I envisioned as lawn, in its place against the view. And when saplings were cleared, branches trimmed and evergreens clipped, the landscape beyond was so extensive, the need for an eye-catcher became evident. Some time after, I found in London the C18th baroque statue of Mercury and Proserpine, a legend delightfully appropriate for its destined setting.

Now the garden-planning started in earnest. The fact that from all around the 'platform' the house sits on, one looks down over extensive grounds dictated a scale that would be readable from above. It was decided to create a 'roseraie' that could be seen from the newly-orientated entrance steps. Eight allées, each a hundred foot long, with white climbing roses trained on iron arches and under-planted with misty blues radiate from a central fountain. These terminate in secret, scented, rooms, or stone stairs leading down to olive groves, or meander up into the three terraces that wrap around the 'acorn's' hillsides; the topmost has pale, sweet-smelling flowers, the lowest, plants that merge imperceptibly into the natural flora. For much of this planting, we drew on the lifetime's knowledge of Claus Scheinart, who had created his critically-admired garden during the several years he lived in nearby Opio.

This vigorous and varied planting is counterbalanced by the utter simplicity of hundreds of olive trees standing regimented in low-walled, mellow stone 'rooms', some of them enlivened by statues of Roman gods and goddesses in the manner of John Cheere. Backdrops of fluttering grey-green olive leaves dappling the grey stone of these eternal figures with sudden stabs of sunlight makes them seem almost alive, while at full-moon they move in a symphony of silver shards. Do Apollo's ears hear the tramp tramp tramp of the legions on the Via Aurelia, does Artemis turn her gaze towards a hilltop temple?

But perhaps one of this garden's most remarkable sights is the astonishingly bold use of Mediterranean cypress. The drama of these most sculptural of trees is an early coup d'oeuil. As the gates open, a seemingly endless avenue of these towering intensely green, flawlessly tended pylons is revealed, leading one up through orchards, and interspersed with paler green youngsters that afford one glimpses of the delights to come. For the gardens at Le Mas are quite simply a delight. They are not drop-dead chic, nor full of gimmicks, not rigidly classic, nor consciously futuristic. They are quite simply right for their environment, their landscape, and their, and our, time. And for that house, happy on its ancient hill.

HEARTS OF DARKNESS

The Literary Review

Haven't we all been there? To that secret place of the heart, that *pavillion d'amour* where, you know, simply know, that someone famously attractive, world-widely desired, is really waiting only for you; just one look, one moment, and you'll be theirs, to look after and love, forever, as no-one else ever has or could? Hear them say, as Joan Didion wrote, "I'll build you a house on that bend in the river where the cottonwoods grow"? Be still, my pounding heart!: it's only make-believe...but...haven't I, haven't you, haven't we?

Well, rarely, these days. Genuine heart-throbs are thin on the ground, or grown gross with age. It's not a question of being merely star-struck. Movie stars are all too visible, rather than blue-moon-papped at El Morocco with Hedy Lamarr on their arm; musicians grunge it in slovenly Shoreditch, not Al Bowley at the Savoy. Glamourous officers in the Senior Services – debs and their mamas swooned for Captain Sir Vyvian Naylor-Leyland, the Dominions for sun-tanned Lieut. Philip Mountbatten glistening in naval whites – are now *invisible*, their sensuous uniforms banned. Artists have become on-show businessmen, whereas Lucien Freud was a shy, sly, heart-breaker at a mere 17. Sportsmen

– think of those impeccable flannels – sweat in lycra; tennis players kick off in big, and black, pants; bless, please, Pancho Gonzalez's little cotton shorts.

Earlier heart-throbs had been literary. Byron, I suppose, but more Heathcliff, Darcy and their ilk. When books became film, it was the actors who took over, pushed by the popular press, and the gradual acceptance of personal publicity. But towards the end of the 1930s , the pin-up of all the world, the Empire's golden boy, was no more. By the blow of Mrs Simpson, he'd come to naught in the eyes of a kept-in-the-dark public, his once unassailable tinselly throne up for grabs by the very kind of men his father so detested him for mixing with.

Many were American...Fred Astaire, Tommy Hitchcock, Shipwreck Kelly, Jock Whitney, and, king of the crop, Douglas Fairbanks Jr. But the US being still somewhat Puritan, they were a wholesome bunch; fast, but not louche. *That* enticing quality was distinctly European, and with an aura of exotic foreignness, rumours of equally exotic endowment, hints of scandal, fast-living, sports-mad, devil may care, there came the all-time heart-throbs...all rich and dark and dazzlingly handsome. Aly Khan, Porfirio Rubirosa, Gianni Agnelli, Dado Ruspoli and Jai Jaipur took the next couple of decades by storm. They had every attribute to set hearts racing, with their planes, their polo ponies, their palaces, their romantic titles...Prince Maharajah, and in the case of Fon Portago, no less than eight leading up to Marquis...to say nothing of the many mistresses they swapped like Happy Families. The label 'playboys' only added to their allure.

There still are desirable sex-objects, but they're too in-your-face, too every day. They don't have the far-away charisma which epitomizes the real heart-throb, the attainability one yearns hopelessly after, plus an infallibility (they might die, and often did, violently, but they wouldn't be ill, or broke), allied to an air of not yet being totally happy, and *needing*...until that one look, that one moment...only you.

MANNERS

An Essay

I'm not sure that manners in a sense of 'etiquette' exist, or even need to exist in today's electronic climate. PC-ness has led to people being cringingly polite, with everyone so bland that they can't have bad manners even by mistake. Black-cabbies have been reduced to pussy-cats because of Uber – though it's absolutely *not on* to shriek at the foreign Ubermensch who haven't a clue where Piccadilly is. Paperless post has removed the pleasure of a personal reply, but it would be polite if the recipient bothered to read to the bottom, and not plague one with what time? And dress code? It's now perfectly ok for *de rigueur* obligations, like bread and butters, to be laptop led; many people prefer this form for important ones, such as condolence letters, and it saves all that box-filing. The crucial thing is to write them.

Bad manners are now far more noticeable in people who aren't aware of the space they take up, and have no conception of people around them...the vast hipster backpacks that send drinks flying, those knots of girls who cluster, vapidly chattering, in doorways, oblivious of anyone trying to get past. There's also a ghastly breed of not-that-young hearties who somehow assume that they are still shit-hot, that no-one but them knows the layout of private jets, roar up to front doors and leave the (loaned) Continental's keys for 'my good man' to deal with, or lounge about, big-bummed, smoking cigars in the Fumoir at Hertford St. If these guys knew how awful they looked slobbering on Coronas they'd quit, sharpish. On the other hand almost everyone on public transport are unfailingly well-mannered, teenagers leaping up to proffer their seats, but I was slightly galled when a near-bald, bandy-legged, very very old lady offered me hers on the bus the other day.

But there are some areas of manners being just plain bad. Not leaving a tip, however small, when you've stayed with friends is unforgivable. Eating popcorn in the cinema is revolting, its stench more stomach-churning than *The Revenant*, and is the current equivalent of the rustling of sweet papers that so infuriated theatregoers of yore. Many of that era abhor using mobiles at dinner. I agree it's fairly boring when obsessively updating, but incoming calls often provide some gossipy juice, and a lifeline when your neighbor has a single subject, cosmetic surgery, schools and hotel-spas having replaced the drone of 'Always take the B349 myself'. Texting is now the only vehicle for a bit of covert flirting, and if 'phone Manners maketh Man', or indeed, girls, I'm all for it.

MY SARTORIAL LIFE

The Sunday Times

'Sartorial' sounds an awfully grand way of describing what I wear. It somehow implies correctness and rigid wardrobe-control. If only either were in my nature, let alone in what I wear. My style, if so it can be called, is a far more haphazard, day-to-day affair. Sartor, it seems, is an alternative word for tailor; but for many periods of my life, I've hardly been conscious of one.

The well-tailored cavalier Beau Brummell, while still at Eton made his classic dictum; only sombre black, white and grey. It remained what we had to wear, but during the tweedy holidays I'd gaze enviously at Teddy Boys in their impudent elegance. On leaving, in the late 1950s I met David Bailey and instantly craved his Mod look – the current street fashion – and was soon getting boxy 'Italian-cut' suits from Bilgorri's in Whitechapel, pointed shoes from Brixton market, and – treasured gift – a narrow, horizontally striped tie, by Jacques Fath no less. A little later, Levi's, then the only known brand of jeans, became available; we wore their stiffness – barely relaxed by bathing in them – with black windcheaters, in emulation of our young Hollywood gods. The die was cast; a whole new way of dressing.

In an essay on Dandies, Max Beerbohm insists

dandyism is one of the decorative arts, that 'to so clothe
the body that its fineness be revealed or its meanness
veiled' is a valid aesthetic aum. Looking pleasing or
interesting to others is making the best of a bad, or
even good, job of the basic material, akin to improving
walls, designing harmonious surroundings, or choosing
beautiful accessories – and also, fundamentally, polite.
I imagine like many people, I have always hated my
looks, longing instead to be a chiseled dark string-bean
rather than a dumpy mouse, and therefore have from
necessity applied a form of decoration on myself as
imaginatively as I have for the many and varied interiors I've designed.

I never had any inclination towards being a dandy
like that arch-practitioner Count D'Orsay, though it
must have been quite fun, for him not least, when
'crowds gathered to see him descend *insolent from his
toilette*', or indeed that handful of exquisitely turned-
out men in 'fifties London, Peter Coates, Bill Aykroyd,
Kim Waterfield (who was indeed always known as
'Dandy Kim') and the gloriously outré Bunny Roger, as
however their style was, it smacked of the archaic.

But I wanted to be up-to-date, aware of advances
in fashion whether street or designer. I've kept my
eyes peeled for changes, and admired the style of '30's
and '40's movie stars, the bowlered pin-stripes of City
gents, the sleek silhouette of continental playboys, the
lumpen scowl of Bovver Boys, the glittered glamour
of rock-stars, the rule-breaking slouch of hip-hop, and,
I'm afraid, often laughably, have adopted them. I'm a
terrible actor, but putting on some other motley gives
me a role of confidence, which maybe is why I had a

ranch in Arizona in the 1960s (show me a guy who hasn't wanted to be a cowboy), have dyed my hair raven (who hasn't yearned to be Elvis?) and even attempted a pathetic imitation of that acme of elegance, the Duke of Beaufort, whom everybody wants to be.

Oddly, I don't now much enjoy actual 'fancy dress'. My heart leaps to my mouth when an invitation decrees Circus, or Star Wars. But it wasn't always so. Soon after leaving school I went to the last ever Chelsea Arts Ball at the Albert Hall as Rudolf Valentino in 'The Young Rajah', a costume consisting solely of a white silk loin-cloth and ropes and ropes of large (plastic) pearls; all well 'n' good, until the mahogany stuff I'd used for an Indian-dark tan leached treacherously onto the pris-tine whiteness, a lesson in however exotic the get-up, make sure it's practical. I was far more comfortable at Bunny's infamous 'Fetish' party, held in 1959, going with a friend who had an absolute thing about police gear; he dressed me in full, authentic, Bobby-on-the-Beat uniform, with pleasing results, I might add. And ever since then, I've underplayed any theme. At a recent 'White Night's' birthday ball in India, where all the guests were elaborately turbanned, I was simpler, in white britches and bum-freezer jacket, hoping it had a kind of Imperial Indian mess-kit look.

I'm sure a major aspect of one's appearance being satisfying to oneself and others is largely clearing unwanted growth. No hairy neck. For that, I'm reliant on Derek Hutchens who has dealt with every phase of my hair at his calm salon *Me* in Abingdon Road since, as my old friend the jeweller Fulco Verdura used to say, before the Anschluss. I never quite know what 'moisturisers' are meant to do, but Sisley's magic men's' skin stuff is a daily essential. And of course, the hygienist, and a regular pruning of all tufty nasal and aural excrescences. And there is a rigidly adhered to 'don't'. Don't ever wear evening studs, certainly not jewelled ones, with a soft-front shirt. They were – should be – only ever used with those board-stuff shirts you can't button. The same goes for cufflinks. I'm supposed to have said they're 'common'. I never did. I maintain they are aging, especially on the young, like cigars. If young guys knew how awful they look smoking them, they never would.

Every day-wise, while I'm not quite such a flibbertigibbet as Juliette de Novembre in Nancy Mitford's *The Blessing* who couldn't think of any occasion without seeing an exact picture of how she would be dressed at it. I do like to work out what might interest/amuse/delight those I'll meet. Notice I don't say impress. That's not part of it, and I dread looking 'distinguished'; rather, 'contemporary', though that covers the contemporary in various periods. Spending much time on building sites, it's overalls and a hard hat, which are greeted with 'Mornin' mate's' rather than sniggers of 'Wot's that woofer doin' 'ere?' And elsewhere, jodhpurs aping Clark Gable's early movies, Robert Wagner's chino'd, loafer'd 50s image, or the pre-war chic of Austrian *tracht*. And of course with age comes more formality. I've used many Savile Row tailors; only one can cut, but all charge the earth – well, around 4,000 chunks of it. Luckily now I've found an exceptional tailor in Hanish, whose deceptively formal-sounding 'Hanish Bespoke Attire' makes superb things executed swiftly and smoothly by his alert awareness of cut and style, and for comparative peanuts, to boot. So now, I go forth more soberly, and though often not adhering to Beau Brummell's strict axiom, I do now see he had a point.

SAIL AWAY

Boat Magazine

'Jolly Boating Weather' we sang lustily at school, but
in my case it was just a half-hearted paddle in a
dodger – I was never graceful enough with an oar to
graduate to a skiff, or was it a whiff? – upriver, and into
a backwater curtained by willows for an hour's illicit
puffing on a Du Maurier. Until then, my experience
on water had been queasy-making trips off choppy
Burnham-on-Crouch in my mother's sloop – she was a
keen amateur yachtswoman, though I think, now, the
keenness centered on her captain. But, once home, and
after a near-death experience in our swimming pool, I
developed a healthy wariness of the deep, believing,
along with Dr. Johnson, that being at sea was like being
in prison with the added possibility of drowning, and a
pursuit best left to Uffa Fox.

But things were to change. The ferry to Capri one
summer dawn in the mid-1950s – that heat-gilded rock
of an island over the prow and Vesuvius wreathed in
smoke behind the wake – awoke the romance of sea
travel, furthered by voyages to and from New York in
various *Queens*, *SS United States*, or the *Isle de France*.
And towards the end of that decade, living in St Tropez,
we would reel out of Ghislaine's, the world's first discotheque, to see Niarchos's ravishing black-hulled *Creole*

had sailed in overnight, or Agnelli's racers, pencil-slim, scudding away below a million sails, and once, Arturo Lopez-Willshaw's fantasy, *La Gaviota*, her decor by Emilio Terry of giraffe-skin-velvet upholstered banquettes, Louis XVI furniture and Ming-potted palms as deliciously, extravagantly, impractical then as it would be today. Off Tahiti *plage* we'd lunch on movie-producer Sam Spiegel's *Malahne* (sister ship of *Shemera*, on which her owner, Lady Docker, had got into deep do-do for tearing up the Monegasque flag) with Betty Bacall and Jean Vanderbilt diving, lithe as ribbons, into the sun-splintered sea.

Don't think for a moment I actually went onboard these fabled crafts, except for Sam Spiegel's. Rather, just gazed, in mute admiration. Later, for one Aegean-sailed August, friends and I hired a leaky tub which soon took on water so alarmingly we had abandoned ship onto Prince and Princess Michael of Greece's gleaming white hull handily towering over us.

My first experiences of actual, grand, seafaring were summer weeks spent on Seymour Camrose and Joan Aly Khan's twin-screw ketch, *Tartar*; loftily flying the White Ensign guaranteed a masthead ballet of dipped burgees, and possibly a welcoming gun-salute, in every port from Salonica to the Costa S'Meralda, where Joan's son, the Aga Khan, had just unleashed his ocean-going *Kalamoun*, arrow-sleek and faster than the wind, on unsuspecting co-racers, while his torpedo-slim *Shergar* gurgled alongside. And moored mountain-like nearby was Adnan Kashoggi's *Nabila*, the original super-yacht, riveting for having an 'Auxiliary Potato-peeler' button in the vast galley, and a handful of yawning young hired to get up and dance when anyone entered the strobe-pulsing onboard nightclub, whether at five or nine a.m. And then there was a bizarre couple named Ricky and Sandra Portanova who were docked – parked-up would better indicate their gaudy galleon's girth – in Monaco: Ricky, no stranger to a tot or two of rum, aroused the ire of Prince Rainier by frequently relieving himself on the steps of the Hotel de Paris, and the banished Portanovas had to high-sail it away to Morocco '.....after all, THAT king lets you pee ANYWHERE', as a Princesse Ghislaine de Polignac astutely commented.

And, as sooner or later everyone must, I discovered the southern shore of Turkey. Initially I drove its length, swerving off treacly tarmac to climb every mountain to ruined arenas, waded out to submerged temples: deep, rippled white marble monoliths more emotive than any museum. And due to divine providence I met Cigdem Simavi, who, with her newspaper-proprietor husband Haldun, had recently founded Gocek, now a world-renowned yacht-haven. Their *Halas*, a 1914 Clyde-built coastal cruiser, later pressed into service for the Dardanelles campaign, was now reincarnated as the last word in maritime luxe for her seasonal stately steam from the Sublime Porte to these calm Carian coastal waters. But Cigdem had her own, far more *intime*, floating pleasure-dome.

Melek was no commonplace *gulet*, but a three-mast schooner, wide-keeled, her only stateroom a sea-going ottoman *divan* of wide low sofas, soft cushions, and furry throws for chillier daybreaks. Somewhere, cheek-by-jowl with bunk-like cabins, was a galley from which Cigden conjured her exquisite Circassian Chicken, or

Black Sea turbot grilled over sweet-scented wood, to be lazily relished before a leap into the limpid depths of yet another turquoise bay, while her handsome sons scampered like tanned acrobats up into the rigging.

That coast was, still is, the most serene to sail along, particularly if one was lucky enough to do so in *The Virginian*, Anthony and Carole Bamford's magnificent...I hesitate to say, merely, boat, as she is also a kind of Aladdin's cave of unexpected pleasures. Fancy a firework display tonight? Whoosh, rockets go up. A zippy dinghy to whizz you to that legendary Kilim dealer? It's bobbing by the side, below. Birthday? Your birthday? Today? Cake, candles, crackers, and be-ribboned presents for a sun-hatter's tea party *just* before dusk.

Equally perfect is the Getty family's sumptuous *Talitha*. Her gleaming white and two yellow-funneled silhouette masks an interior filled with rare maritime art and incunabula found by Christopher Gibbs; and being slightly smaller than *The Virginian*, *Talitha* can slide gracefully between the narrowest of headlands. Victoria, model-trim in a couture rubber diving suit, plunges fearlessly into the violet depth, emerges, towels off, and leads the way, for drinks, to a lonely, whitewashed Seljuk basilica shading a far earlier temple's scattered columns. On leaving *Talitha*, your tender makes a full circuit of the vessel; above you, the immaculate crew lines the gunwales, saluting. It's a parting that can't fail to induce sweet sorrow.

One summer in Corfu, we looked out to sea and Albania had been blotted out by a movie mogul's liner sized love boat. Asked aboard, and stepping off the vertiginous gangplank, our salty sore eyes were met with the sight of a three-story-high fully-equipped gym, with oiled blonde bodies flexing like muscle-bound mermen. Up several storeys, along miles of bland wood corridors we encountered a child, wandering, lost, who whined "When are we GETTING ON the boat?" After an hour's tour, we were ushered into a panoramic saloon. At the far end, dressed for an opening at the Met, was Nora Ephron, ordering martinis.

And so to now...at least, for summers past. Omer Koc's *Messeret* has streaked out of Bodrum under an inky, star-spangled arc, and one awakens in the lee of an isolated Greek island to a breakfast of sizzling omelette and plump mangoes with that unique sweet-sour cream – Omer's Turkish chefs not only make the Lucullan food, they write best-selling cookbooks. Later we will swim ashore, maybe find that one *taverna*, or the goat-path to a strange, slightly sulphurous spring, once bathed in, who knows, by gods. Pale pink wine passes the sleepy afternoon's sail to a further island, possibly Patmos, a grand dinner up in Chora, entailing much 'Do we REALLY have to dress?' Well, no. You can stay on board and watch a '40's movie, ask for another carparinho, or be massaged by any of the many-skilled crew *Messeret* conceals amidships. One, a gentle Russian giant, tells me 'water energizes the body'. Surely that's one good reason we love being at sea.

WARHOL

Harper's Bazaar

Andy. Always Andy, under that glittering spoon-fed moon; hair a froth of silver, askew, anchored, neat or long, Asian or synthetic. Andy, always Andy: symbolic, more New York than the Empire State, more American than the Rockies, the more so because he had wrenched the U.S. from its mid-century comfort zone, and stuffed its cherished emblems down throats and up Park Avenue harder than a stevedore's sledgehammer. Andy, always Andy, and there on that banquette the beautiful, the blasé, the bloodsuckers and the starstruck...the Nans and the Frans, the Dianes and the Dianas, the euro-trashed and the dollar princes, their images etched by strobe, in acrylic, on celluloid and even in piss, from Perth to Peru.

Actually, I only saw him a few times in that satin-shorted, drug-drooling, acid-dropping scene. I'd skedaddled to Arizona, California, London, by the time the bouncers and Bianca held sway. But I knew he was there, always. Who didn't?

* * *

He was hovering over the desk of Kay Hayes, Vogue's shoe editor, who had a good claim to have 'discovered' him. He had a mousy fringe, the pallor of youth, watchful eyes and a portfolio. Out of it came marvels. Witty, exquisite sketches – my God, the boy can draw like, no, better than, Schiele. The sure line, the paint-box colours. Where, how, did he learn, this geek-child of Ruthenian immigrants? Where, in banal Pittsburg fringes, was that talent nurtured to explosion? What had he seen, clocked, copied, or was it, quite simply, genius? At suppers at his mother's house way uptown, Lex and the '80's? I never asked. She couldn't have said. It was a mystery to her too.

Later, in a Baco-foil wrapped warehouse, cameras turned. Andy mumbled, hustlers humped. It all began to go bad. Not bad as in off, or BAD, man, as in good, but bad like forbidden fruit. Everyone wanted to touch it, eat it, drink its heady nectar, be part of it. Andy's natural reserve, and, yes, modesty, held the gropers and gawpers at bay up to a point, but then glamour, that fatal flower, opened wide and exposed his world; not in emperor's clothes, but in the pied-piper livery and Kodakolour and Vistavision and 3D. The Factory fraternity was spot-lit as both saints and sinners, not an easy role for anyone, least of all Andy who hid behind those still-watchful eyes, wonder and wistfulness and billions deep in them. The Factory went into overdrive, the prices sky high.

* * *

Andy, always Andy. The silver moon has long since set, the spoon recycled in the blue bin. The foil has tarnished, the 'new' Factory dining room, scene of lunches

180   NICKY HASLAM

power-housed enough to make Arianna Huffington
huff, has closed its high double doors. Art has become
an essential, not a caprice, all too often a trivialized version of Andy's originality, and decades after. But after
Andy? Andy, always Andy.

DIARY

The Spectator

I was once bundled into a police car in Palm Springs to explain why I didn't have snow-tyres on my pick-up in the red-hot California desert. I don't remember the outcome of the 'arraignment', but will never forget the lady cop's name, L. Nevada Yonkers. Other weird names have stuck with me. Reading *The Most of Nora Ephron* – whom I met once and immediately fell in love with – I realised that when I was working on *Vogue* in New York in the 1960s, she had been on the staff of *Newsweek*. I used to be obsessed by the weird names of the girls on *Newsweek*'s masthead. I would reel them off like a litany. I can still recall Virginia Bittikofer, Minnie Magazine, Olga Giddy and, best of all, Fortunata Snyder Trapnell, whom I stalked vicariously through several marriages and divorces. Of course, the lately deceased Duchess of Alba's string of names took the biscuit, but with the grim news that Doris and Edna are suddenly fashionable, I rather long for a return to, say, Marie-Anna Berta Felicie Johanna Ghislaine Theodora Huberta Georgina Helene Genoveva, the given names of my friend Countess Esterhazy, who is known – understandably – as Bunny.

The other Bunny — Roger — used to give brilliant New Year's Eve costume balls. Now that everyone is fed up with the looming 'Happy Holidays' by October, and bankers have themselves a Merrill-Lynchy Christmas by bailing out of London weeks before it comes, it would be hard for a host to gather a houseful of friends to see the year out in the style Bunny achieved. His invitations, greatly coveted, were coded. 'The Enchanted Will Meet in Another Part of the Forest' read one, cryptically, and 'Miss Norma Desmond, At Home, 10086 Sunset Boulevard' another. Guests clad as movie stars arrived to find Bunny's house transformed into that film's decaying mansion, and the host a ringer for its star, Gloria Swanson. But the last, simply saying 'Fetish', lived up to the name, and led to several famous people being papped in most unseemly dress in the frosty street, their embarrassment front page in the *News of the World* next day.

A lad who works in Bond Street tells me about 'mystery shoppers'. It must be boring enough to have to deal with people who intend to buy something, but these are spies who pretend to be customers, sent to see if the service is up to scratch. They arrive, apparently as obvious to the staff as A.A. Gill in a restaurant, and have to be constantly Sir and Modom'd as they poke about, ask for things in different sizes and colours, then leave empty-handed. Mr Grace would have had none of it.

Three months into a driving licence-free year, I'm now a Tube-a-holic, and though my comprehension of the local station, Earl's Court, is still rather haphazard, I'm struck by the daintiness of Underground English. 'Please alight here for...' must sound awfully airy-fairy to foreigners. And 'the next lift arriving *shall* be...' would please Fowler, but wouldn't *will* be more reassuring?

From dainty to dopey... those maddening cod-philo-sophical HSBC ads lining the slipway to the plane. And now there's a huge building site at South Ken. blaring yet more ludicrous aphorisms by an artist. 'Nothing is impossible. Nothing is possible. (Even nothing changes)' and 'All my ideas are imported. All my products are exported. (All my explanations are rubbish)'. I'll say.

Let us hope, vainly I fear, that there will be fewer saddening memorial services this year. But even the most moving had its funny moments. At Mary Soames' memorial service, turning round against the tide of departing mourners in the Abbey's aisle to greet the venerable Clarissa Avon, Antonia Fraser, Harold Pinter's esteemed widow, was barred by a badged church-gor-gon hissing 'Make way, Lord Hurd is coming through.'

Needing new songs for my cabaret at the St James's Theatre (slotted for late April) my pianist said some-thing up-tempo was needed, and suggested one of Ethel Merman's from Irving Berlin's *Call Me Madam*. I remember Arthur Laurents, who wrote *Gypsy* for the Big Belter, saying that when Sondheim told Ethel he had a great song for her, 'Everything's Coming Up Roses', she looked puzzled and asked: 'Everything's coming up Rose's what?'

Addendum to above, top. Due to a painful toe, my GP sends me to 'the best foot man'. The genius's name is Dr Mallipeddi. You couldn't... as they say.

NOTEBOOK: A SEASON
OF LAUGHTER & SADNESS

The Spectator

This summer brought highs and lows, sadness and laughter, some irritating, some exhilarating. I was fortunate to be uplifted by an encounter with Leslie Bonham Carter, a remarkable woman who seems quite British but is in fact American. She is the daughter of Condé Nast, who founded the company that bears his name. He was born 145 years ago, in 1869. Leslie witnessed the full glamour of 1930s America. When the First World War came, many British grandees packed their children off to America. Young Leslie had opposite plans. All she thought of was how to get to England, to be there in its darkest hour. Diplomatic strings pulled, she sailed, barely in her teens and without either parent, in a battleship across those sub-infested waters. At 8.30 on the morning of 8 July 1943, she 'saw my first sight of England ... the England I have talked, thought and dreamed about ... the England I love'. Over 80 years later, despite its glaring faults, Leslie loves it still.

The death of another ardent lover of England has cast a pall on this summer's lushness. Candida Lycett Green sought out, explored, and wrote about almost every building, lane, turret and copse, horse and cart throughout the land. She wore her knowledge lightly but she cared passionately — both traits she inherited from her father, John Betjeman. She created rooms, houses and gardens that were a miscellany of colourful vividness and gentle erudition. Her parties — and there were many — though planned to a T with her adoring family, had that ineffable ingredient, spontaneity. And then the beauty, the raucous laugh, the lack of swank or self-pity. Some years ago, on a holiday, I was moaning about a slight upcoming cancer operation. Of course she didn't mention she had that devilish affliction herself.

Believing in Satan has disappeared from our current psyche. No churchman dares mention him. His disturbing image, that horned and tailed creature, is portrayed throughout the ages. Oh, we think smugly, surely he never existed. But perhaps he does. While on a boat in Greece, I read *Imaginary Creatures* by Jorge Luis Borges, about weird beings rooted in legend. Most of his work is way over my head, though these monsters are fascinating to any numbskull. Were they entirely 'imaginary'? Or, over centuries, did word of mouth describe what had once been alive? The Djinns — the Muslim creed's version of devils — appear as smallish shapes of a fire-like substance that evaporate suddenly into an outline of sparks. A recent David Attenborough documentary showed deep-sea creatures apparently doing exactly that.

My charming friend Alicia Castro, the Argentine ambassador, had pooh-poohed my claim, half-remembered from a long article on the author in the *New Yorker* some years ago, to be related to Borges. Dear old Google proved it true; Jorge Luis was born

Borges-Haslam. But his grandmother, Fanny Haslam, from Lancashire, really was a cousin of my dad. It will be the red carpet at the Casa Rosada, surely.

The co-writer of this magazine's bridge column, Janet de Botton, played a trump card at dinner in her Provençal paradise the other week; Bette Midler was there. So was her charming husband. Though Bette's screen persona is huge and flamboyant, she is petite and almost puppy-like in appearance, with the most perfect skin, and darting, beautiful, expressive hands. Wildly funny and self-effacing at the same time, she drew the best out of everyone round the table, encouraged revelations, and added many of her own about the biz of show — particularly that Michael Jackson didn't talk with that breathy squeak but in a perfectly normal baritone.

Talking of baritones, after some recent in-depth radio news coverage on Israel/Gaza, the presenter announced 'Now, a comment on the situation by Princess Anne.' We heard a sensible, cultivated, measured voice speaking surprisingly knowledgably for several minutes. Then the presenter said 'Thank you, Prince Hassan.'

A fellow guest at a wedding in Northern Ireland this weekend was the artist Mark Adlington. Anyone who has not seen his astonishing paintings of otters illustrating the re-issue of Gavin Maxwell's *Ring of Bright Water* should dash to Daunt's. One, of a torpedo-like otter streaking forwards, followed by a shimmering wake, is quite extraordinary.

A NIGHT LIKE THIS

A Preface

For *Bosphorus Private* by Nevbahar Koç

Someone said "….and here the ladies of the Seraglio, the beauties of the Empire, would trail their diaphanous silks over the water, their bejeweled fingers glinting, alluring to the fish below"……

……we were on a boat, motionless under a starflecked night, in a bay in the lee of the Asian shore. We looked down; a shimmer of quicksilver scales, the lightning flick of an arrowhead tail verifying, just below the velvet surface, the presence of a shoal, curious for a moment, then darting, deeper.

The boat moved noiselessly now, its wake scarcely a dark path between moonlit ripples. A fish leaps, twirls, and falls, a watery comet….. 'and there were kiosks, in carnation gardens, set among those woods,' someone else was saying, pointing ahead, 'and the Sultan's family would come, as evening fell, to this refreshing coolness in the summer nights'.

A summer night like this. We were on our way to a pre-wedding feast, sumptuously laid out before a pale yellow yali set above the shoreline. Agile boatmen hand us up onto the dark dock, the slap of water against stout timber abrupt, staccato! after our calm voyage. Now we can see the thronged terraces, lit by myriad candles of amber wax. Then, through gauze-swathed doorways, chandeliers illuminate immense tables bearing all manner of Turkish delights, among them those self-same fish, curled and sauced now – their pinkish flesh retaining a silvery sheen – set amid crimson pomegranate, the porcelain-white of petal-sprinkled labne, the glow of quinces, the turbans of sesame-seeded gevrek.

'Do look. Over there' someone says, gesturing towards a group on a sofa and a long-necked figure, elegant in black, and pearls, and a tremblant diamond rose. 'She is the last Ottoman princess; born in Dolmabahce, that palace with the crystal staircase, a month or so before the sultan abdicated'. I watch this unique, vivid link to Istanbul's imperial past, her aquiline features, her deep, dark eyes, her silver-grey hair, for several minutes. Had she, as a very young girl, I wondered, floated gently across the Bosphorus while fish shimmered around her kayigi, and violet dusk faded into star-flecked heavens? As indeed had I, a mere hour – or is it a lifetime? – ago, on a night like this.

ONE MAN'S MEAT

The Literary Review

A review of *The Last Playboy: The High Life of Porfirio Rubirosa* by Shawn Levy

LL RIGHT, ALL RIGHT, I know. I know what you're dying to know. How big was it? Well, Shawn Levy doesn't give the answer precisely in feet and inches, but quotes several ladies and one or two gents who were quite literally gobsmacked when the custom-made, palest-blue, monogrammed Sulka boxer shorts came off. One wife, Doris Duke, compared it to 'the last foot of a baseball bat'; another wrote that Rubi was 'grotesquely proportioned', and that it 'could have been a carnival attraction'. Truman Capote made a sighing stab at sizes, while Jerome Zerbe, more accustomed to photographing the members of El Morocco, described it as 'Yul Brynner in a black turtleneck'.

I mention this somewhat indelicate subject first because I imagine it's about the only thing people now associate with Porfirio Rubirosa. This riveting, often very funny book should put paid to that, as it focuses not only on the breathtakingly bold materialist manoeuvres of this sensationally attractive man ('fair-skinned enough to pass for Latin as opposed to Negro') but also on the Dominican Republic of his birth, as ruled by the murderous, conniving and appallingly cruel dictator

Rafael Trujillo – whose son, Ramfis, a poisonous lout
with perhaps even more vicious tendencies than his
father (they had political opponents lowered alive into
vats of boiling oil, and we are talking late 1950s here,
not the Crusades), was for many years Rubirosa's pro-
tégé. It is the biography of not one but three Creole
autocrats.

Trujillo was not overjoyed when the young lieu-
tenant Rubirosa, moulded into the superbly fitting if
somewhat Ruritanian uniforms which were de rigueur
for his corrupt Caribbean court, began an affair with
his daughter (the exotically named Flor de Oro), for
whom he'd planned a more international future. He
insisted they marry immediately. The deflowered Flor
noted during her honeymoon, 'my insides hurt a lot',
and though no child was conceived (in their combined
thirteen marriages, neither Flor nor Rubi had children),
Rubirosa as legendary lover, supreme seducer, irresist-
ible stud – the cause of those smutty sniggers about
peppermills – was born.

Soon Trujillo twigged that dazzling Don Porfirio and
Señora Flor de Oro Rubirosa Ariza could be a handy
bit of PR for his banana Reich (it hadn't cut much ice
in more sophisticated salons that, so far, only a Haitian
gossip column had described them as 'the best-dressed,
best-educated couple in town'), and packed them off,
with a few vague diplomatic credentials, to the Berlin
of the 1936 Olympics. They were fêted by Goering, and
sat in the Führer's box; 'I have admired the great work
of Hitler', Flor wrote dutifully to Papa, adding 'I'd like
you to transfer us to Paris'. En route, the Rubirosas
represented the Dominican Republic at the coronation

of King George VI. En poste in Paris, the fun really began for Rubi, if not for Flor, who, after he had been implicated in a dodgy jewellery heist in Spain and the botched murder of a Dominican dissident in New York, found her priapic husband, in more ways than one, rather too much to take. Back in Ciudad Trujillo, divorced and often under house arrest at her father's orders, she would dismiss Rubi with a shrug, answering those who asked if he was handsome or charming with a curt 'For a Dominican'.

Danielle Darrieux, the leading film star in occupied France, didn't feel that way at all. Following Rubi to an internment camp in Germany, she pulled a string (in the form of Joseph Goebbels) and pretty soon, in Vichy, became the second Señora Rubirosa. While the war curtailed Rubi's involvement with his former father-in-law's domestic policy (Trujillo had recently slaughtered some 20,000 peons), he managed, in the words of his brother Cesar, to 'get rich selling visas to Jews. Didn't everybody?'

The tainted money enabled Rubi to evolve into the famous figure the world's press came to extol. Fabulously handsome, impeccably mannered, immaculately yet unconventionally dressed (the first to wear jeans with a blazer, loafers without socks), he was the ultra-charming, uber sportive, polo-ponied, Ferrari-driving, machismo male of every woman's fantasy. The author describes that just-postwar world – particularly the Parisian one – with a joyous freshness, but never fails to remind the reader, in passages which read every bit as chillingly as Vargas Llosa's The Feast of the Goat, that the monster of violence back in Ciudad Trujillo

was keeping a blood-soaked finger on Rubi's move-
ments. Simultaneously, the US State Department, fear-
ing another Cuba-like Communist debacle, was playing
a double game of subterfuge versus aid, and kept a
sharp eye on the murderous Goat, his brutal kid, and
the suave, roving 'ambassador'.

Shot of Mlle Darrieux, who'd probably found that
being Mme Porfirio Rubirosa Ariza wasn't the only
thing about their union that was too much of a mouth-
ful, Rubi moved into the big time by marrying a young
reporter who came to interview him. Handily, she was
none other than Doris Duke, 'the Richest Girl in the
World', a headstrong though extremely generous lady
with great taste and a very large mouth. It sounds as
though they were genuinely happy, though Stewart
Granger noted that she made him dance attendance
on her. He danced for fourteen months then changed
partners, to Zsa Zsa Gabor; this time it was impure
pleasure. 'I cannot be without him. Rubi is a disease
of the blood', was Zsa Zsa's garbled Hungarian way of
putting it. Together they hit every playpen and nightspot between Los Angeles and Rome. Levy's account of
Rubi's vastly aroused passion is delicious Hollywood
Fifties froth, what with Zsa Zsa roping in her friend
Kim Novak as a sex-toy for Ramfis Trujillo.

The flies in the ointment were that Zsa Zsa was
not only married, she was high-maintenance. Putting
her on the back burner, and 'broke', he claimed, from
gambling, Rubi provoked the headline 'RUBI NABS
BABS' with a new marriage. Beautiful, sensitive and sad,
Barbara Hutton was the one truly tragic passenger on
this ship of fools, and was predictably dazed at her fifth

voyage down the aisle – one wedding guest noted that 'the bride wore black Balenciaga and carried a scotch-and-soda'. The marriage lasted, equally predictably, just seventy-five days. Rubi, garnering about $24 million in today's dosh, went back to Zsa-Zsa, and, taking acting lessons from Michael Chekhov (the nephew of Anton, no less), tried to become a film star himself.

These spot-lit shenanigans were carefully monitored back home. After twenty years of raping and killing his countrymen, Trujillo in decline was still as violent; the US government showed interest in the disappearance of several well-known dissidents; and the psychotic Ramfis, with his new tactic of slicing off eyelids, was on the ascent. Rubi – rich, high-flying, adored – was still 'the most valuable asset' the old dictator had on the world stage, and friendship with the new regime in the White House was required. Rubi became a pillar of that Camelot court.

He may have flirted with the Kennedys, the Cassinis and the Sinatras, but then he married the young French actress Odile Rodin. One could never have accused Rubi of 'slowing down', but with Odile he became somewhat quieter, though he still ran with the pack – Taki Theodoracopulos, Günther Sachs, Sammy Davis Jr, the Duke and Duchess of Windsor, Joe DiMaggio, Christina Onassis, the Niarchoses, the Rothschilds, and his greatest friend, Prince Aly Khan: they were the Beautiful People. And thus it's a disappointment that the book contains not a single illustration.

If it did, there would surely be one of Rubi's Ferrari slammed into a tree at eight o'clock one golden summer morning in Paris with his crumpled body inside.

But maybe this flamboyant figure, flawed, fun, chic, courteous, sometimes wicked, often notorious, but always loved, must be seen as Shawn Levy paints him – wholly fascinating.

U OR NON U

The Oldie

No, this isn't about that, though I'm sure Muv would have fainted and Farve reached for the entrenching tool if any of their 'rowdy girls', as a contemporary described them, ever suggested further education, little enough basic having been foisted on them as it was.

But we all know that despite this, each in their own way became leading figures, albeit leaning rather right, in the C20th they spanned. Theirs was not an age when many girls went to university; if they did, it was to one the two established English places....no wallflower deb worth her salty tears wanted to be shunted off to St Andrews. One feels the few that followed their light or dark blue brothers saw it as kind of Oxford-bagged or punt-kissed pre-cocktail party to the cocktail parties in nightly white-tied London ballrooms, or gazing at the Prince of Wales in the Embassy.

Trouble is, the New Universities were considered rather.....well, I'm afraid to say...non U. There was a pause of almost six hundred years until Durham was founded, and after that, due to Industrial Revolutionaries' thirst for education and ritual and leadership, a whole slew of gloomily-Gothic and shiny magenta-bricked seats of higher learning soared skyward. Even so, young

men the country wide aspired to the Real Thing....
my father, born in 1887 to a Bolton cotton-spinning
burgher and schooled at beefy Sedbergh, went up to
King's, mingling with rather more greenery-gallery
figures like E M Forster or James Elroy Flecker, and
his lifelong friend Maynard Keynes, before the diplomatic service. (His brother Robert, the first male pupil
at Bedales, was to be a much-married and somewhat
dilettante architect, which kinda proves this particular
pudding). My own brothers were expected and did follow in illustrious Cambrian footsteps, although thereaf-
ter having lacklustre careers in things like insurance; in
my case, general dimness precluded my doing so. Wits,
and perhaps even wit, had to suffice. Knowing that Mrs
Hutton paid the orchestra at her daughter Barbara's
coming-out ball $20.000 extra NOT to play "I Found
a Million Dollar Baby in a Five and Ten Cent Store"
seemed to say as much about financial proclivities as
any Keynesian Principle.

By the 1960's it was becoming de rigeur to go to
university, whether to indulge in further Bullingdon
buckery or settle down to serious scholarship, with
both, in many cases, following the blueprint of their
forebears. But there is clearly a difference between
deep-seated erudition and almost unconsciously-ac-
quired knowledge, looking out rather than inwards.
'Travel broadens the mind' provided it's the mind that
travels, discovering different interests than the prosaic
subjects.... classics, philosophy, physics, law, etc, of
university tradition. Clearly, these are absorbing to true
scholars, but they run the risk of being known to be
clever, and, living their life in an intellectual bubble,

anxiously compare themselves to, and often smugly dismiss, those with better degrees from other – not necessarily better – universities. The non-Uni goer tends to wear knowledge lightly, and display it – a supreme example being Paddy Leigh Fermor – with anecdote, detail, humour and humaneness.

Many of the contemporaries I admire didn't opt for University, perhaps thinking that knowledge, dangerous or otherwise, could be something advantageous soon rather than late. Yet each in their chosen fields has become top of their particular tree. Algy Cluff has cornered oil, Simon Robertson is this country's foremost, and most-respected, banker; Min Hogg, by founding The World of Interiors, opened all eyes to the breadth and depth of decoration. Besides being a seriously good painter, with her quicksilver mind Lindy Dufferin has transformed a ravishing but tumbledown estate into leading agricultural/dairy production. Janet de Botton – though having easy entrée into either Oxford or Cambridge as her Wolffson grandfather is one of only two men to have a college named for him at both (the other is Jesus) has scored in highest maths as an international bridge champion. Sir John Richardson, now 94, is assuredly the world authority on C20 painting. Adrian Gill and Bryan Ferry were at art schools before forging their stellar, totally different, careers. Above all, Christopher Gibbs, who, after a somewhat profligate post-Eton, grew to knew everything and more about any form of human artistic creativity, past and present, from architecture, paintings, carvings and furnishings, to books, porcelain, and textiles, knew the history of who made them and where for, and whether or where they still existed. He conveyed this all-embracing knowledge with a gentle, of almost wistful, touch, allayed to his profound absorption of all religions, let alone an even softer touch in persuading many of his friends to donate massive sums to cultural institutions. The latter could hardly have been learned at any university.

Well, perhaps it could, these days. In the now-prevalent headlong stampede to university, any university, there may well be a course in philanthropy along with those in, say, Ethical Hacking (Dundee), David Beckham-ry (Stafford) or Pizza Hut Studies (Manchester Metropolitan) especially as now there are agencies like All Answers that will write the personal statement for you, albeit, it seems, somewhat clumsily. But even that doesn't hinder acceptance at universities Kingdom-wide. Going up has become the norm, but it would seem the quality is going down, becoming merely a means to that all-important symbol, a degree. Let's hope there are still independently-minded young who will say NON! to U, and realize that a lot of this currently-vogueish, uniform, 'knowledge' can be a dangerously dull thing.

SAN LORENZO

Tatler

There are, of course, restaurants with famed signature dishes...Claude Terrail's Duck à l'Orange, Cardini's Caesar Salad, Oysters Rockefeller at Antoine's, say. But one didn't have to fly far in those pre-bucket-shop days of the 1970s to order the hors d'oeuvre that was to put Mara Berni's on everyone's lips.

Bagna Cauda was a gloopy greyish warmish brew of essentially, I think, stock, cream, olive oil and pounded anchovies, with bits of whatever the kitchen had to hand that day flung into the mix. And, when the contents of a basket of the chewier raw vegetables was dipped into it and lifted, carefully, to the mouth, wow, a new taste: Mara had invented, at least for greasy-spoonfed Londoners, crudités. And San Lorenzo, named after Mr. Mara, and, incidentally, the patron saint of chefs, took off.

How did they do it, these two wonderful-looking young Tuscans? There were already a slew of Trats dotted around; Italian cuisine was making inroads into Elizabeth David's Francophile dicta. But those restaurants were in trad areas, Soho, the King's Road, Mayfair, so to plonk for dainty Beauchamp Place – then known as Bankruptcy Row, infamous since the '30s for selling

Chippendale-ish pine mantelpieces – and what's more to set out their stall in that tiny shed in a patch of garden behind an anonymous doorway, was, to put it mildly, risky. But Lorenzo and Mara Berni had seen it, and come, and conquered.

The premises quickly expanded. A glossy entrance, then an interior staircase designed for making one. Overnight, it seemed, a new glassy area, jungled in greenery, would be added, and each in turn became the place to be placed...Mara had a narrow roster of favorites. The menu, Bagna Cauda aside, wasn't in truth all that original. It was, however, served with a kind of off-hand elegance, always by glamorously raven-haired waiters with whom it was soon fashionable to have an affair; some became boutique gurus.....Piero di Monzi....or designers, and some, if they dared a Berni balling-out, leaving to open their own, but never rivaling, versions.

A bar was created, and a 'private' room upstairs, usually the kiss of death in dining terms, but where Mara, who incorporated the role of confidante/comforter in her already sorceress-like persona, would console weeping wives and jilted playboys. The stars, the younger royals, the rockers, the models, flocked, though generous foreigners...this dinner's on me.... scusi, ancora Pino Grigio, ...were often mortified to find no credit cards were accepted, and in those ATM-less days, cash whip-rounds were a norm. It was all part of the dégagé charm, a charm dished up by Mara and Lorenzo and their beautiful children (with whom it was extremely fashionable to have an affair) that made one feel honored to be there, thrilled to be allowed to gawp at the glamorati, and when Mara came and sat at one's table….. Well!

While other restaurants fell by the wayside, San Lorenzo stood the test of years, or at least for a good three decades of them. Now, though essentially the same, with the odd new dish added to the tried and true, it has become, like many of its clientele, something of a period piece. This hasn't diminished its charm, or even its originality, though the old guard, for whom it was so long a temple, have dispersed to foodier pastures. But go, and you'll see Lorenzo, burlier now, keeping his well-trained eye on the proceedings, and if you listen carefully, amid the tap of texting, you can still hear Mara's siren-song, and you'll ask, like Princess Diana, for the Bagna Cauda.

LETTER TO MY YOUNGER SELF

Attitude

M aking contact with that youth of so many decades past is akin to throwing a pebble into a
deep cave and hoping to hear the faint ping
of its reaching the dark caverns below. There may be
an echo, the trace of a young voice, but time and tide
have erased any ripple of clarity, and memory, such
as it is, can hardly be considered reliable. To exam-
ine the persona of the *me* of so long ago would need
a microscope of as yet undiscovered strength. We all
know that youth rarely listens to its elders, let alone
having any intention of taking what advice they may
proffer. The expression pissing into the wind comes to
mind. Maxims for a successful adulthood are instantly
blown back straight into the face of the giver.

I knew precious little of 'youth' for most my early
youth, except for my immediate surroundings and its
household. What with my father far too old, and my
brothers too young to fight in it, the war had held the
outside world at bay, and then, just after it was over,
getting polio meant several years of almost exclusively
adult contact. There was no-one of my own age to
share youth's normally budding knowledge, pleasures
or pains. It was in some way just assumed one would
grow up to be happy, intelligent, straight, healthy and

capable. It really wasn't till my early teens that I realized there was whole new world of beauty, music, sun and sex.

So it may be better to switch the roles, while remembering the vast timespan that separates them, and try to gauge what that faraway voice might have to say, laugh or shudder at, criticize or have pride in, even have faint praise for the person at the well-head. Here we go...

Why weren't you more inquisitive in those days? Details are what make life fascinating, fleshing out the history one's grimly taught at school. Why didn't you ask your parents, or any adults, about the momentous times and dramatic events of *their* lifetimes...the murder of the Tzar, the rise of Hitler, the Abdication, Hiroshima, for instance? Answer: one dreaded the voice of grown-ups banging on. One shouldn't.

Why were/are you so quick to accept any invitation? To a party, to write an article, to a picnic, a wedding in Istanbul, to send something, to do a chore or favour, without first thinking if you can, and then have to go through agony trying to make good, or get out of them. Well, enthusiasm is a step in the right direction.

Whatever made you wear such ridiculous, corny, often too-young clothes? I tend to believe the point of fashion is to be bang up-to-date, and the trouble is I've always disliked my given appearance. Prefer to be a chameleon. And, as Gertrude Stein noted, 'one MUST be modern'.

Why didn't you take more care of things you were given? That celluloid cartoon of Snow White, autographed, from Walt Disney, for instance, or the Andy Warhol painting he'd signed for you, or letters from

Cole Porter? I suppose, then, one didn't realize such things would become so wildly valuable. And the letters were stolen.

Why do you still leave everything to the last minute? No excuse.

Why did you give up learning to play the piano? Ditto, with laziness added.

Why do you get more critical as you get older? I'm afraid I see more to be critical about.

But you do have one or two good traits. Apart from cigarettes, you don't have an addictive personality... not to drink, or drugs, or pain, or sex and rock 'n roll. You're quite good with people, and can usually find something fascinating or funny even in the most tedious bores. That goes for children too, but that's probably because they're not your own. And you have a good retentive eye and ear for places and conversations.

People always trot out the old cliché 'Life's too short'. But really I think life is actually too *long*, however long, to harbor grudges, to continue rows, to feel slights, or rancor at people falling out of love with one. It's best to realize early on that one cannot control love. It's maybe there, somewhere, someday, and may come again. So I tend to pin hopes on a lyric in a Jimmy Van Heusen song.....

'Makes you think, perhaps, that love, like youth, is wasted on the young'.

ILYONA IN IDLEWILD

A Diary

Until a sullen wing of rain shivered onto it, the garden on La Cienega glittered invitingly, brazen as costume jewelry. Emerald-plastic topiary, gleaming faux stone. I am doing book signings, L.A style, and it's still only 11 a m. Central Casting jocks, cling-wrapped in monochrome livery, passed frosted smoothies to the haut and bas of Angelino design, brave new seekers of Hollywood's grail. The squall has hurried all under cover: wisps of steam writhe round the dark denim thighs and ivory chinos in my eye line.

Through this grid of limbs, for a split second, I see a slight, exotic vision. A `Salome' by Gustave Moreau, perhaps, wrapped in a billow of puce, some by-gone houri of the Steppes. Pulled-up, crimson-lake hair, and plate-like hat tipped forward over the whited face, carmine lips.

Then the thighs reconfigure, and she's hidden. I uncap the Sharpies. 'Tell me who to, please'......

'May I speak viz you?' She's there, at my side, little taller than my chair back. I turn. See the violet pallor of her cheek, the questioning arched brow, the sanguine mouth. 'Do you mind if I speak viz you?'

Er...'No, not at all'.

'Ve are going to be friends!'

OK, but what with? A Transylvanian, for cert.

'Great friends!' Like a dare.

'Romanian?' I'm channeling Mme Lupescu.

'No! No! No darling!... (deep red mouth wide over daz-white teeth)... Hungarian!' The second syllable is a hiss. 'But I live in Idlevild! Do you know it???'

'Well, it used to be New York airport when I was...'

'No darling! Idlevild here, above Palm Springs. I haf home! High on mountain! I haf ice! I haf snow! I look over burning deserts!'

Sounds like Baked Alaska I think but don't say.

'You vill come visit me? My name is Ilyona von Z......'

'I'd love to'. I would, too.

'You vill come? Ve vill be happy.' A silence. 'Tell me! Do you know my friend Princess M.....???? You do! She vos jus here, viz me! Ve write, ve talk, ve gaze, ve laugh, ve write more, ve eat, ve talk! Jus here, viz me! In Idlevild!'

She leans closer. 'You vill come viz me for lunch tomorrow?'

'I'm afraid I can't'.

'Why not? Day after, zen! Day after?'

'But I leave for San Francisco'.

'You vill not be going! My card......'. And she glides away.

* * *

Curiously enough, I didn't leave that day, having copped a quite severe dose of food poisoning. So I call Ilyona to say this will certainly prevent us meeting this trip.

'Food poison! Oy Vey! Where did you eat?'.

'Oh, er, a hotel on Sunset'.

'I know zat hotel. Terrible! Horrible people! Ladri! And vot, may I ask, did they serve you?'

'A forty-five dollar hamburger'.

'Oy Vey! Hamburger! Most un-vise!'.....admonishing pause....'Hamburger! Dead! I haf not eaten dead flesh for years!'

And the telephone goes TLCK.

THE PRINCE OF WALES

The Daily Telegraph

I t is quite possible that today nobody knows what Prince Charles is really like, not even Prince Charles himself. For seventy years he has needed to devote his time and energy into not being himself, for much of it in a position in which nothing private should show. It is hardly his fault that his lifetime has seen the erosion of such privacy; the quid pro quo is that, understandably, he shows his feelings publicly.

He was born with great sensitivity and a quick mind, both of which are still his characteristics, and to which have been added an instinctive kindness, an insouciant sense of humour, and above all, being historically minded, a passionate, if sometimes over-traditional, knowledge and respect for every field of the arts. In some cases his opinions, often initially pooh-poohed, have been shown to be spot-on; others deemed faintly cranky, but his is not a conventional mind, and his outspokenness adds elan to national debate.

Prince Charles has two parents who are supremely good at their jobs. There is almost nowhere in the world they haven't been, nothing, on almost every level, they haven't experienced or enhanced, and they are globally loved and respected. Hence there are far fewer opportunities for the great statement, the grand gesture.

Nonetheless, the Prince of Wales has crafted his own unique persona. The last prince to bear that title had, if fleetingly, a new, c20th world at his feet. Prince Charles has, with subtlety, originality and tenacity, kept the 21st at his elbow. He knows, and comments on, what he likes and admires, and equally what upsets or irritates him. In this, he is most surely his own man, and a man of his time.

GILDED YOUTH

The Spectator

A review of *I Read the News
Today, Oh Boy* by Paul Howard

There was a touch of Raymond Radiguet, the young literary sensation of 1920s Paris, about Tara Browne. In life poetically beautiful, poetry-imbued, tender and trusting, deliciously precocious and eerily presumptive, androgynous in looks but not desires, Tara died – 'without knowing it', as Cocteau said of Radiguet – tragically, but given his penchant for very fast cars, unsurprisingly young. And like Radiguet having touched the lives of those who knew him with a kind of iridescence that remained with them, more than half a century later. This lengthy biography which, given its subject's foreshortened life is necessarily somewhat repetitive, has gathered their still-vivid recollections, and if it reads more as a protracted tabloid double-spread, that's the fault, and expectation, of our times rather than the author's, or Tara's.

His childhood milieu included the Irish writers and English aristocrats, mondain Parisians and questionable New Yorkers who peopled his divorced parents circle. His philandering father, Lord Oranmore and Browne, newly married to the film star Sally Grey, had given up the fortune-depleting task of farming a vast estate in

Galway for the safety of Eaton Square. Tara's mother Oonagh, most elegant of three Guinness sisters, had recently become the wife of a gay, soi-disant Cuban depleter-of-fortunes named Miguel Ferreras. Oonagh adored children; more looked unlikely from this union, and as her youngest, merely five at the time, Tara was destined to become the apple of her strange grey eyes, her companion, her confidante.

In many ways, Oonagh is the central character in this story. If one can safely say that all members of the legendarily rich Guinness brewing dynasty, whether born (and often if married to) one, are a uniquely self-obsessed clan, it seems not true of Oonagh. Willful, sometimes steely, she nevertheless has a self-effacing, even shy, personality, preferring to let others gambol in – and often pushing them into – the limelight, allowing her fortune to make those around her happier. She inevitably spoiled Tara, but it was the form of spoilage intended to bring out the best in him. Oonagh also handed Tara, on a silver-gilt plate, her innate generosity, loyalty, and elegance of appearance.

I witnessed, once, the latter in its most dazzling form. I was dancing at Ghislaine's, the known-world's first discotheque squeezed into a cellar behind the fish-market in St Tropez. Actually, to drop a name, I was dancing with Bardot, but somehow there came the message that Oonagh was on her way. I went and sat waiting in Senequier, watching, as far across the bay, a pale dot became a Riva; closer, the paleness shimmered into Oonagh and Tara, both in narrow white, both white-gold headed, standing, laughing, holding glasses; a spot-lighting moon dappled the water around them.

With the engine still chugging, Tara leapt, turned, and whirled his mother lightly onto the quay. It was like some balletic pas-de-deux, two ethereal water-sprites touching down on mortal stone. Then they ran, human now, towards the thump of 'Hit the Road, Jack'. Tara was, I suppose, about fourteen at the time.

There was, of course, no hint of conventional education. Tara baulked at Eton, lasted a few weeks somewhere less rigid. Mixing the Martinis for Oonagh's friends filled up the remaining 1950s, and it was hardly his fault that LSD took over the ensuing decade and the set he was party to, particularly the new wave of young music makers, or that he was privy to the LSD that allowed it be so seemingly carefree. While he was – fatally – a dab hand at souping-up sports cars, at one point owning a garage in Bayswater to do so, his slight, velvet-clad figure was the leading light in London or Luggala, his mother's Gothic getaway deep in the Wicklow mountains...he and Ireland seemed exotic in those more insular times. And girls fell headlong, several still remembering Tara as their first great love. That he should instead fall for and marry a slip of a local girl with much the same silhouette as his own was a blow to many, his parents included, and if Oonagh's insistence on rearing their two children as her own seemed harsh at the time, in hindsight it gave them, after Tara died and Nikki's problematical life, a stability they might not have otherwise known.

The devastating, particularly to Oonagh, crash that killed him has become near folkloric, not least because of the Beatles song that is the title of this book. But for the many people who read the news that day, Tara

is alive and golden, beautiful and poetic, somewhere
deep in their hearts, today.

VANITY FAIR AND FOUL

The Spectator

People tend to use the term 'Fashion Victim' somewhat damningly – and maybe jealously – to
describe someone obsessed by the latest look.
I'm not sure I agree. There's something endearing
about anyone who wants to dress in the newest style,
and anyway, isn't being up-to-date the whole point
of 'fashion'? It's no more reprehensible than wanting
the newest car, or iPhone, or flattest TV. 'Victims' are
surely those who get it wrong, the mutton and lamb
syndrome; more like what my beloved friend Melissa
Wyndham called Fashion Casualties.

But now Alison Matthews David has brass-tackled
the subject. In *Fashion Victims: The dangers of dress
past and present has* shown in gruesome detail many
fashions that did, still could, hasten their wearers to
untimely deaths. We've heard about arsenic in St
Helena's green wallpaper poisoning Napoleon, but not
that our Victorian forebears were swathed in the same
toxic stuff, in clothes, shoes, feathers and artificial flowers. Who'd have thought that our parent's boots were
blacked with benzene treated with fuming nitric acid
which causes the extremities and lips to turn back from
cyanosis....the very same concoction 'used extensively
in dry cleaning'.

In my youth, little girls in tulle dresses were always going up in flames, but it's alarming to read that today's rampant slogans on even the most respectable brands of T-shirts are made from *nonylphenol exothalates* that, when washed, leach deathly chemicals into the rest of your laundry.

If you sport your grandpa's topper at Ascot, chances are it's embedded with mercury, heralding 'a pus-filled rash on the forehead', let alone 'impeding your intellectual faculties'. And ladies, be wary of celluloid hair-combs, a popular EBay item. Our wall-of-glass windows magnify sun's rays, which can explode these recycled accessories into your scalp. Even the confidence-giving white coats of doctors harbour lethal bacteria including *Staphylococcus aureus,* our old friend MRSA. Nanny was dead right about catching your death, and not only of cold.

Stitches in Time...The story of the clothes we wear by Lucy Adlington is for geeks rather than victims; this informative journey through essentially workaday clothing and its more decorative elements, tells how garments evolved and developed and why some have lasted. Its no-nonsense tone is slightly marred by weak puns ('Reaching New Heights' is a chapter on high heels). I looked in vain for a reference to the stuff of the Wee-Willy-Winky-style nightwear of my childhood, linsey-woolsey, which I'm astonished to find one can still E-buy today. Must be safe as houses.

In *The Fine Art of Fashion Illustration* Julian Robinson reveals what great artists fashion illustrators, from the Renaissance until eclipsed by C20th magazine photographers, really were. The details of dress in the author's selection... simple, ravishing or ludicrous....are deliciously depicted, and show how close is the relation of painters to illustrators, particularly in the late C18th, and vice versa. Watteau's nephew Francois-Louis-Joseph drew as exquisitely as his uncle; some figures on these pages could be by Boucher or Gainsborough, others recall the diaphanous 'attitudes' of Lady Hamilton, or knock spots of Tamara Lempika. It's intriguing to look at these illustrations, each specifically dated, and picture their subjects in rooms – rustling silks in Kedleston, say, or stridently deco against Syrie Maugham's all-whiteness – of the various periods.

Matthaus Konrad Schwartz was born in Germany in 1497, becoming, age 23, chief accountant to the billionaire Fugger family, famously inventors of banking. His portrait by Hans Maler hangs in the Louvre. Though stylistically typical of the early C16th, the degage sable stole and multi-tasseled shirt strung with necklaces hint at a degree of dandyism.

As well they might. From age five, Matthaus had himself painted each time he ordered a new outfit. On parchment, with a printed text on how and when and why he wore them, and made from, they were bound into a miniscule (10x16 cm) book, and it has been enlarged by Ulinka Rublack and Maria Hayward into *The First Book of Fashion. The book of clothes of Matthaus and Veit Konrad Schwartz of Augsburg.* It's quite simply the most fascinating record of a 'victim' one could hope for.

In August 1518, for archery, Matthaus is in restrained monochrome, enlivened by gilded trellis-work hotpants Liberace would've killed for, but by May 1521, he's into scarlet ostrich feathers and armour, over a red-stripe silk-satin onesie 'to walk towards His Highness Ferdinand of Austria', and beside it, handwritten, 'The face is well-captured'. On May Day, 1528, he goes shooting in peach taffeta knickerbockers, the 'doublet like gold and pearls sparkling'. By 1539, its 'pure white half-silk' top-to-toe, and, thriftily, it being only half-silk, he had 'an identical black outfit made".

In July 1526 Matthaus is painted starkers, front and back views, as 'my figure… had become fat and round'. It hadn't, but it's nice to see he wasn't vain. And there were no flies on him either: his codpieces, spherical or upturned – he wore 'the bag-style just once' – are modishly adorned, and while his outfits become faintly more sober as he ages, his son Veit Konrad's veer toward the prosaic. The authors point out that many forms of new materials were flowing into Europe at this time; mirrors became more than court luxury: never has the mold of form been reflected in the glass of fashion as entertainingly as in this scholarly work.

FALSE PERSPECTIVE

The New York Times

There's a story that Marella Agnelli, on first seeing a friend's silken-velvet-walled, frankly-French C18th-style 5th Avenue apartment, gasped, as if for air.... 'But don't you just LONG for a bit of wicker?' These words come back to me every time I see yet another 'authentically' conceived room, you know, the exposed brick, poured concrete, the reclaimed wood, the glare of unrelieved glass. In such surroundings, Signora Agnelli, who, it should be remembered, created a 'minimalist' décor years before its perpetrators were born, would have as readily longed for something humdrum, something witty, something inappropriate or even frankly fake to – well, – take the curse off such sanctimonious sterility.

Of course, it's that word 'fake' which makes people's hackles rise. It implies ersatz, second rate, meretricious. Fake sounds a little less contemptible when rebranded as sham, pretended, or imitative, but takes on an even more respectable connotation when upgraded to 'inspiring', being the development of an original concept, or seeing that object as being something to which to add a new concept of beauty or zest. As if by sleight of hand, 'fake' is transformed into influenced by, revisited, given a new twist.

I live in a 'sham' Gothic (sham Jacobean actually, but let's not split definitives) house of extreme whimsical delicacy, but even the grimmest of minimalists fall for its 'fake' facade. A diamond Cartier feather is, au fond, a fake feather, but I doubt that any severely pro-authenticity proprietress of those soulless spaces would throw one in the trash. Madame de Pompadour had the flower-beds at Versailles replanted during dinner with thousands of 'fake' porcelain flowers, thereby not only ensuring constant work for the Sevres manufacturers, but also their creation of ravishingly beautiful artworks whose rarity value today is incalculable.

When the few seams of the world's more exotic marbles were exhausted, 18th C architects had craftsmen all over Europe paint the equivalent, but if one suggests a unique marbleized finish to the authent-a-crowd, they shudder and beetle back to boring calacatta. Fake is surely only contemptible when it's trying to pass as original, when quite simply forgery, or counterfeit. But a witty take on the real thing is a different matter. Fake fur springs to mind.

Many years ago I decorated an apartment for a client who had an outstanding collection of contemporary art. His neighbor, oddly enough the nephew of Col. Gaddafi, saw this interior, and requested an identical version, art and all. My team and I spent several happy evenings knocking up Stellas and Rauchenburgs and Fontanas, which, while not trying to be fakes or even 'homage', were things that brightened up the un-jaded young Libyan's life (though our task might have been made simpler if the collection had included Basquiats or Twomblys). Conversely, my sister, who was married to Mr Brillo and collected rather tougher artists like Leger, was deeply – and regretfully – unimpressed when I showed her the early work of my young friend Andy Warhol, deciding the last thing she needed were fake fakes of her husband's product.

I suspect that the 'authentic' is really taste for people with no taste. One can't really criticize that exposed brick wall, the steel supports, the rough stone. There's nothing *wrong* with them. They were, are, the essential lynchpins of the human need and desire to build. But new materials, substances, and surfaces develop taste; it seems quixotic to willfully disregard their aptness and usefulness and charm, determining instead on an industrial austerity which appears to be effortlessly simple, but which once achieved is blandly static.

The Golden Age magnates, ordering all their (usually, paradoxically, fake) furniture from Paris, along with walls-full of Old Masters from Duveen, had zero intrinsic taste, but a lingering memory of, and yearning for, European culture. It remained so until Elsie de Wolfe came along to inject a bit of decorative frivolity into those gloomy 1890s mansions. Her style caught the public's imagination like wildfire, and her innovative lightheartedness set the style for the first half of the coming century, as, among the things De Wolfe insisted on in this 'new' world, was an acceptance of new materials. Just as in previous centuries royalty had been thrilled to await the latest-discovered woods or Chinese lacquer to be incorporated into their newest furniture, so De Wolfe introduced the most up-to – date materials... plastic, Bakelite, spun glass, acrylic, nylon. All these were to influence not only interior design...

Dorothy Draper, Billy Haines et al, but artists – think Dali – fashion (Schiaparelli), magazines and most of all, film sets, but to turn fake into a valid art form. As the incessant millions spent acquiring a Warhol, the grand old man of the art, prove, there's nothing so authentic as a fake.

THE INFLUENTIAL TOUCH
OF A VANISHED HAND

The Spectator

A review of *Nancy Lancaster: Her Life, Her World, Her Art* by Robert Becker

One evening in the mid-1930s Nancy Lancaster, at the time Mrs Ronald Tree, dined with Lady Colefax. Among the guests was the future Duchess of Windsor. "Could you be the same Wallis Warfield I saw walking down Franklin Street in Richmond, Virginia, wearing a monocle and spats?" She was, and now there is a photograph, taken in 1914, of Wallis wearing this bizarre *tenue* in Michael Bloch's newest book on the Duchess. Mrs Lancaster's total recall not only of this arresting vision but the place, time, and conversation surrounding it is typical of her gimlet eye and vivid memory which form the nuggets in this book's rich seam.

These two women shared nearly identical backgrounds. Well-born Southerners, both with a passion for decoration and stylish living. Both married English grandees, both lived ever after in a kind of exile, the Duchess's from *force majeure*, but Mrs Lancaster's was willingly self-imposed; and whatever the triumphs of her art, the successes of her life in an adopted country, and a world which adopted her with open arms, it was for the rural, post-bellum-Virginia of her birth and her innate American roots that she, unlike the Duchess, secretly yearned. Yearned for Mirador, the estate where she was born and which she eventually owned and heartbreakingly had to sell; yearned for Misfit-- - prophetic name---Mirador's marching property, the first house she ever bought.

If the Duchess had a totally modern outlook, Mrs Lancaster was *au fond* nostalgic, a sentiment she vehemently denied possessing, but nevertheless its implication in Robert Becker's masterly chronicle of her volatile character and near-intangible life is inescapable, and ultimately deeply moving. Mrs Lancaster's influence on C20th decoration, decorative architecture and indeed garden design is now widespread — if relatively unsung — and this book puts that influence in its true perspective. The bands of ragging-dragging gypsies probably don't realise that without her long-remembered and later-recreated paint recipes, our walls would be a blanket of Dulux Magnolia, and Cheltenham lady decorators unaware that, had she not brought chintz downstairs, curtains would still be a dingy-colour rep, four inches off the floor. But it's more than that, of course. Her taste, if not Mrs Lancaster herself, is a direct link with the 18th century, a culture that fortuitously hibernated in the industrial-revolution-less southern United States of her youth: her evocation of that time is in many ways the most fascinating part of this book.

Though rustic, Virginia was no back-water. Scions of English families constantly shot and hunted its blue-hilled valleys; beautiful Nancy's legendarily beautiful aunts and sisters married those scions. Such unions,

particularly the Astor one, gave Nancy instant entree
to the highest society, coupled with her own to Anglo-
American Ronald Tree. That world, hating change then
as much as now, warily clung to draughty, powerless
corridors and comfortless rooms, and lives war-death
saddened, servant-problem ridden, blown apart by debt
. . . or Detmar Blow. There had been a few sidelong
glances at the gilvered glamour of Sassoon-style chic, at
the white lacquer and looking-glass of Mrs Maugham
and Lady Mendl (for whom a Mirador was a quite
different thing), but Nancy's knack of reinterpreting
convention, of reapplying the 18th century's technique
with a totally fresh eye, of breathtaking comfort and
light-enhancing colour, provided a new yet traditional
formula that calmed patrician nerves. Her own magnificent houses and those she decorated for friends —
('Decorators, if they are any good, get very intimate
with their clients') — were her showcases and it was
not until the dazzling partnership with John Fowler
that she actually became a business, decorating for a
wider swathe of clients, among them the by now mon-
ocle-less Wallis, and establishing a style that became,
and still is, even in its watered-down and plagiarised
form, the most influential decorative trend of the 20th
century.

Robert Becker — perhaps willy-nilly---lets Nancy
Lancaster speak her life. Little use is made of diaries or
letters in his text, which consists of her recollections
and theories, her own idiosyncratic voice presented in
great chunks of bold type. It is a satisfying device, for
it allows the reader to `hear' her character, humorous
and wistful, dictatorial yet receptive, feel her boundless

stamina. Above all, while grateful for her English life, she remained deeply proud of her Virginian stock (a Confederate flag always flew above her English houses) and of a South before it became soap-opera hackneyed. And when, in an article, I described her famed yellow library as 'Buttah-Yellah' she was on the telephone in a flash to remonstrate. 'We don't talk in that common Southern accent". But although she says in this book 'I can only just read and write' what poetry there is in her spoken word, especially of the colours she loved:

'Hardly pink . . . white like the white beneath a shadow . . . dirty dandelion....not brown or black or the usual grey, but the colour of a dead mouse; the soul of blue---with candlelight, it filled up the room like a mist'.

Her art, her intrinsic tie to past beauty and excellence, is vivid on every page; her world, and the way her world lived, equally so: granted, her first marriage proved that Trees really do grow on money, and few other couples, however rich, can have shipped several horses, carriages, tack, grooms, maids, cooks, chauffeurs, valets and children across the Atlantic and back several times a year. The creation of Ditchley must have cost an incalculable fortune, with gilding and gardens, furniture and objects, paintings and parties and pleasure. That it was not labelled nouveau riche (Tree's was a Chicago department-store fortune) is due to the 'off-hand perfection' that Cecil Beaton noted. As Nancy modestly puts it, 'I can mix things, it's the one quality I have.'

And yet, and yet, there is the underlying sadness. Almost no reference is made, but the Tree marriage fails ('I wish to God that you were my brother') and the next, to Jubilee Lancaster, barely recorded....'I'm no good at husbands, but I can find butlers.' Her children are hardly mentioned, and while her relationship with her aunt, Nancy Astor, is lovingly described, one realises, as she did, that it is the houses and the furniture and the servants that are her real friends.

Others have written that this book is the history of a life as the subject would like to have it believed. Maybe so. Nonetheless it is a riveting document, and anyway, we all know history is bunk. In Nancy Lancaster's case, the bunk would be an Elephant's Breath-painted four-post bed, trimmed in palest snuff-coloured silk, on a verandah, overlooking a lilac-scented garden. At Mirador.

HOW TO GET ON AT
5 HERTFORD STREET

A Poem

With apologies to John Betjeman.

Lord Normanby doesn't 'do' fish-knives
And his phone's off – it won't make a sound
The starched damask napkins aren't crumpled
As there aren't any Kiddies around.

When it gets a bit rammed in the bars, love,
The Courtyard's the place you should be
And Michael will soon take your order –
But did you, *really*, say 'G'n'T'?

Robin's constantly tweaking the decor,
But wants to know what's being done
With those portraits of dukes by Sir Oswald –
Rifat's gone and hung in the john.

Are the regulars all down in Lou-Lou's?
The fillies and studs there can't wait
For Garret's next transgender evening
To find out that 'girl's' their best mate.

No, *don't* use a fork for your fois gras!
Do use the banquette for your dog,
And Christian will get it a cushion
And with any luck give you a snog.

Be glad Lucy's riding in Shropshire
Or she'd have you thrown out, you can bet
If she heard you complain 'There's no doilies'
Or demanding a 'fresh serviette'.

You can ogle Farage in the Smoke Room
Banging on about all those Re-moans
He may be the new face of gentry
But he still calls the *brioche* a scone.

Sir, you really must wear a jacket
And can't take it off if you're hot.
I know what I wanted to ask you...
Are you a member or not?